GREEN

One Pound Meals

PHOTOGRAPHY
DAN JONES

DESIGN
SUPERFANTASTIC

GREEN

One Pound Meals

www.miguelbarclay.com

CONTENTS

If you've read one of my books before, you'll know there are no chapters. Just flick through and find something you fancy, or take your pick from the list below.

INTRODUCTION

It's such an amazing feeling to be sitting here writing my seventh book, and I'm so grateful to every single person who has bought a book in the past, and also to those of you who have just discovered One Pound Meals. Without you, none of this would have been possible. I was extremely lucky in the early days to get a book deal and have the opportunity to write down the recipes in my head, but that was just the first step. Without actual physical sales, it would have ended at book one. Fast forward a few years, and I'm still going! Who could have predicted that?

The initial spark that created this series of books was my Instagram, and I know a lot of you have discovered me through the recipes I post on there. Instagram Stories is my test kitchen: it's where I document the process and how I get to the final book. So check me out on Instagram (@miguelbarclay) and see how it all happens behind the scenes.

I'm so proud to be introducing this collection of recipes, all with a green theme. It feels like a natural next step in the series and a nice progression. I like to flick through my previous cookbooks and see how my recipe writing has evolved, and with all I have learned from the past six books, I think this could be the best one yet. I hope it will be a useful book that you'll want to use every day at home.

Miguel

WHAT EVEN IS 'GREEN'?

Green is a word we hear thrown about a lot these days, but what do we really mean by it? The general vibe we're going for – and the philosophy behind this book – is that green is 'good', both good for you and good for the environment. It's about making choices about the things you do and the foods you eat that will benefit you and the world around you. There is no doubt that attitudes are slowly changing: more and more people are becoming passionate about making changes in their everyday lives and striving to contribute towards a greener world. But just a small step or a slight shift in attitude is all that is needed to kickstart something much bigger. Give it a go and see where it takes you.

GREEN FOR THE ENVIRONMENT

The environmental impact of what we eat can no longer be ignored: the planet is suffering, and farming practices are a huge contributing factor. So one thing we can all do is be more conscious about what goes on our plates. Simple substitutions all add up in the long term to help reduce the impact we make.

Livestock farming in particular has a huge environmental impact, so this book has been specifically written to help you incorporate more veggie options into your weekly routine. By making it effortless, fun and tasty, you won't even miss the meat – and you'll be on your way to embracing a new, more plant-focused approach to mealtimes.

And if you still enjoy your meat, like I do, never fear. I have included some recipes that contain meat, but I've used clever swaps, like using chicken instead of beef in a chilli con carne, as the environmental impact of this meat is smaller. As minor as this swap may seem at first glance, it really does all help. In fact, if everyone made changes like this, the cumulative results would be ginormous. So don't get too hung up on the £1 budget – that's not the primary focus here. Why not treat yourself to less intensively farmed, free-range, higher-quality chicken? Let's be flexible in our approach and just do what feels right for our individual situations. The blueprint of how to cook the dish is written down, and you can make whatever adjustments you like. Plus, to help give you even more inspiration, I have also included veggie swap suggestions for you to try out.

GREEN TO SAVE FOOD

Another topic I want to tackle in this book is food waste. In the UK alone, households waste 4.5 million tonnes of food every year. I want to look at that and suggest ways that we can reduce food waste in our own homes. Even things that you might assume can't be used, like vegetable peelings or banana skins, can be turned into delicious meals. I hope I can help you become a bit more conscious of the food that you may be throwing away, and I'll do it by providing you with some brilliant ideas and tasty inspiration, from using up herb stalks to a slightly more adventurous banana peel pulled pork substitute (really!).

GREEN ON YOUR PLATE

And we're not just looking at green foods from an environmental perspective. Eating green also means enjoying foods that are fresh and seasonal, with a 'just picked' and 'straight to the plate' ideology that is so much healthier for you than processed foods with all their preservatives. In this book, stodgy meats and heavy carbs have been replaced with healthier vegetables as the hero ingredient, helping you feel better and more energised. It's all too easy to see green food as a side dish or just a token bit of green on the side of a plate – instead, try to make at least half of your plate fresh veg. From using lettuce wraps instead of tortillas to replacing meat with cauliflower, this is a much healthier and more vibrant way to approach your meal times.

SIMPLE SUBSTITUTIONS ARE EASY

One of the easiest ways to approach a change in your diet is to keep cooking your favourite familiar dishes, but just swap one ingredient. Drastic changes in your daily life are harder to commit to and don't have the best chance of sticking. So let's do something easy. For example, instead of bacon in a carbonara, why not try my smoked paprika-dusted aubergine swap (page 70)? It's easy to make and tastes delicious, plus you get the added health benefits of not eating bacon. (I still love bacon, by the way – I just eat it less often as I gradually phase meat out of my diet.)

ONE POUND PRICE TAG

Just like with my other books, all these meals can be cooked for £1. Invariably there will be leftover ingredients, but by overlapping ingredients between multiple recipes, the blueprint to using them up is already set out – just keep flicking and find a new aubergine recipe that takes your fancy. I've tried to include handy tips for different recipes that share the same ingredients so you can cook both in the same week and use everything up.

EASY TO DO

It's not just about price: by limiting yourself to £1, the recipes become much easier and less daunting. You can glance at the ingredients list and realise you're just a couple of ingredients away from giving it a go. That is the key to how I have managed to inspire so many people into cooking my recipes – don't give them an excuse to say no! If you like the photo, you can cook it tonight.

PORTION SIZES

I've also gone back to the heart of One Pound Meals, with most of the recipes in this book serving one person. One of the things I noticed most from my previous books is the shift towards cooking for one. Times have changed over the past 10 years, and people's circumstances are different. People have come to really appreciate recipes being written for one person. Plus the maths is just so simple: if you want to cook for more, just multiply by the number of people. I have also included a few recipes for four, but that's just because those particular recipes work out better when cooked this way, like my Chicken Shawarma & Butter Rice (page 108), which is more of a special 'feast', or my Whole Squash Pasta (page 120) that uses an entire squash, including the skin and seeds – it just makes sense to use the whole thing up. But don't worry, if you ever cook too much, you can just save your leftovers for the next day.

MIGUEL'S GREEN MANIFESTO

So we all know we'd like to do a little better, be a little greener, but it can be really hard to know where to start. There's so much information out there and it can be a bit overwhelming. That's why I've decided to put together this little 'green manifesto' of small and achievable changes we can all make, in the kitchen and on our plates, that will help each of us make a difference. There are no rules, just keep it fun and see if you can push yourself into a greener way of living.

PLAN YOUR MEALS

You don't have to be super regimented about this, but thinking about what you'd like to cook before you go shopping each week can help you avoid food waste and make sure you pick meals that share similar ingredients so you can use everything up. It can also stop you from making those ill-advised hungry spur-of-the-moment decisions in the supermarket!

MEAT MONDAYS

How about flipping Meat-Free Mondays on its head to change your mindset? Instead, try having meat only on a Monday (or you can choose a different day) and eating plant-based throughout the rest of the week.

VARIETY IS KEY

So much of our food comes from the same old familiar plants and animals. So let's try to add a greater diversity to our diets. Instead of chicken and potatoes, give foods like polenta, couscous, parsnips, barley and asparagus a go.

SAY NO TO PLASTIC

It's always so sad to see unnecessary plastic packaging being used. I know that sometimes it is unavoidable, but on the whole this problem has really got out of hand. With simple adjustments to your thinking, like grabbing loose fruit and veg from the big crates instead of choosing the pre-packed stuff, you can make a difference to your impact on the environment. Plus, with this particular example, there is also the benefit of purchasing exactly the quantity you need, and therefore avoiding waste.

Another nice trend that has appeared in the past ten years is the use of reusable bags and the decline of the old supermarket plastic bags: this has been an overwhelming success and is certainly a huge step in the right direction. I was very surprised at just how easily this change in attitude came about, and I think it shows promise.

RECYCLE

Get in the habit of rinsing out and separating tins, jars and cartons as soon as you're done with them so you can put them straight in the recycling. If you have any packaging that can't be picked up in your usual recycling collection, check at your local recycling bank before throwing them in the general waste.

AVOID FOOD WASTE

This is perhaps the most obvious, but also the most under-appreciated way to save both the environment and your money. Simple things like checking the fridge before you go shopping or freezing leftover ingredients are easy to slip into your routine, but in this book I've taken it to the next level with ideas like pakoras made from vegetable-peelings (page 72). It might sound extreme, but why not give it a try? Just have some fun with it.

EAT SEASONALLY

We all know that asparagus is an expensive luxury, but during the asparagus season the price plummets and there are shelves and shelves of asparagus in the supermarkets.

This is when you should capitalise and eat so much asparagus that you don't even want to eat it again for another year. That's eating seasonally, and that's how food is supposed to be consumed: we should be celebrating foods when they are in season, not flying them halfway around the globe.

DIVERSIFY THE SEAFOOD YOU EAT

Sustainability is a huge issue when it comes to the fishing industry, and in essence it all boils down to varying the seafood you eat. If everyone just ate one type of fish, this delicate ecosystem would be in huge trouble. So, look out for sustainable fish and vary your diet – and maybe look further than the usual cod, salmon and tuna.

EAT LOCALLY

Let's try and save some air miles and find out what the suppliers on our own doorsteps have to offer. Instead of flying in green beans from Kenya, let's see if there is a local food market or a greengrocer selling locally grown veg. Go on an adventure and see what you can find; ask a few questions and see where it takes you.

(ALMOST)* ALL THE RECIPES ARE FOR A SINGLE SERVING

IF YOU'RE COOKING FOR MORE THAN 1, JUST MULTIPLY THE INGREDIENTS.

* Because this book is all about being green, there are some recipes where the most low-waste way of making them is to make more than 1 serving. So for those ones, you'll want to invite your mates over.

PESTO BRUNCH EGGS

Adding the pesto before you fry your eggs means it incorporates into the eggs as they set, giving you delicious pesto-infused eggs: perfect served for brunch with some potatoes and spinach.

To make 1 portion

1 potato, chopped into 2cm dice (no need to peel)

1 tbsp shop-bought pesto

2 eggs

A few cherry tomatoes, quartered

Handful of spinach

Handful of grated Parmesan cheese

Olive oil

Salt and pepper

To cook

Preheat your oven to 180°C/gas mark 4.

Spread out the diced potato on a baking tray. Drizzle with olive oil and season with a pinch of salt. Roast for about 20 minutes, or until cooked through. Remove from the oven and set aside.

Place a frying pan over a medium heat and add the pesto and a glug of olive oil. Break in the eggs and add the tomatoes (keeping the tomatoes on one side of the pan, away from the eggs). Once the eggs are cooked, remove the pan from the heat. Add the spinach and potatoes to the pan and mix everything together. Once the spinach has wilted, season, then serve topped with a sprinkling of Parmesan cheese.

OVEN-ROASTED MOROCCAN VEG & COUSCOUS

Couscous is such a versatile ingredient: it can take on strong flavours and pad out veg to create a main meal. Ideal for picnics and packed lunches, this is a great recipe for preparing in advance.

To make 1 portion

½ red onion, diced

½ red pepper, diced

½ courgette, diced

½ carrot, diced

¼ mug of couscous

½ tsp of cumin

Small handful of raisins

½ mug of boiling water

Small handful of flaked almonds

Small handful of chopped parsley

Olive oil

Salt and pepper

To cook

Preheat your oven to 180°C/gas mark 4.

Spread out the diced onion, pepper, courgette and carrot on a baking tray. Drizzle with olive oil and sprinkle over a pinch of salt and pepper, then roast for 15–20 minutes.

Meanwhile, put the couscous, cumin and raisins in a bowl. Pour over the boiling water and leave for 10 minutes so the couscous can absorb the water. Fluff with a fork, then mix in the roasted veg. Season to taste, add a splash of olive oil, and serve garnished with flaked almonds and chopped parsley.

SCALLION PANCAKES

With just a handful of ingredients, this is how to make something from nothing. If you want to make the pancakes really flaky, then there is a little bit of extra effort required to create those layers, but it's totally worth it.

To make 1 portion

75g plain flour

50g water

2 spring onions, sliced, plus extra to serve

1 tsp crispy chilli oil

Salt

Vegetable oil

To cook

Mix together the flour and water in a bowl along with a big pinch of salt. Transfer the mixture to a clean worktop and knead until it comes together to form a dough.

Briefly pan-fry the spring onions in a big glug of olive oil over a medium heat for about 1 minute (and I really do mean a big glug: use about double what you think you should use). Set aside and allow to cool.

Rub some oil on your worktop and squash out the dough to make it as big and flat as you can – aim for a rough rectangle of about 30cm x 10cm. Spread the spring onions and their oil over the dough. Roll the dough lengthways to create a thick sausage, then chop into about 6 sections. Turn each section so the cut sides are on the top and bottom, then squash each one flat with the palm of your hand.

Using the same pan you used for the spring onions, pan-fry the pancakes over a medium heat for a few minutes on each side until golden brown. Serve with some crispy chilli oil and some more sliced spring onion scattered over the top.

ASPARAGUS FRIED RICE WITH A CRISPY EGG

You can throw almost anything into fried rice and get amazing results, so why not asparagus? I like to dip asparagus in a runny egg yolk, so here, instead of scrambling the egg like you usually do with fried rice, I thought it might be nice to fry the egg and stick it on top.

To make 1 portion

¼ onion, finely diced

1 garlic clove, finely diced

A few spears of asparagus, sliced into chunks at an angle

Handful of leftover cold rice

1 tsp crispy chilli sauce, plus extra for garnish

1 egg

Splash of soy sauce

Vegetable oil

To cook

Pan-fry the onion in a splash of oil over a high heat for a couple of minutes before adding the garlic and asparagus. After about 2 minutes, as the garlic starts to colour, add the cooked rice and crispy chilli sauce, then continue to pan-fry for a few more minutes. Scrape everything to one side and crack an egg into the empty side. Fry the egg to your liking, then add a splash of soy sauce to the rice and give it a stir. Serve the rice with the fried egg on top, along with an extra dollop of crispy chilli sauce.

Tip

If you don't have any leftover rice, then simply pop ½ mug of rice and 1 mug of water in a saucepan with a lid. Cook over a medium heat for about 10 minutes, then allow to cool (you need to let it cool before frying or it will go mushy).

TOMATOES ON HUMMUS

Adding roasted cherry tomatoes to *anything* makes it better! They have just the right balance of sweetness and tartness to elevate even the simplest snack to the next level.

To make 1 portion

Handful of cherry tomatoes

Pinch of dried oregano

2 slices of sourdough bread

2 tbsp hummus

Olive oil

Salt and pepper

To cook

Preheat your oven to 180°C/gas mark 4.

Throw the tomatoes into an ovenproof dish. Drizzle with olive oil and sprinkle with salt, pepper and the oregano. Roast in the oven for about 20 minutes until soft and gooey.

Drizzle the sourdough with a little bit of olive oil and scatter over a small pinch of salt, then place in the oven, straight on the wire shelf, for the last 5 minutes of the tomatoes' cooking time. You want the bread to be toasted and nicely brown.

Spread the hummus on the sourdough toast, top with the tomatoes, then drizzle over any juices from the dish you cooked the tomatoes in. Serve straight away.

> **Tip**
> If you don't think you'll get through a whole loaf of sourdough while it's fresh, slice it up and store it in the freezer so you can just take out one slice at a time to defrost or toast when you need it.

CHEESY LEEK-STUFFED MUSHROOMS

Really quick and easy, this is a huge shortcut to some delicious food with only a few ingredients. The key to this dish is to use a fine grater to create a fluffy mound of Cheddar that will combine with a splash of cream to create a 'no-cook' cheesy paste. It's also a delicious way to use up any stale bread you have lying around.

To make 1 portion

Small handful of finely grated Cheddar cheese

Splash of single cream

2 portobello mushrooms

Small handful of chopped stale bread

A few thin slices of leek

Handful of rocket

Olive oil

Black pepper

To cook

Preheat your oven to 180°C/gas mark 4.

Place the finely grated Cheddar in a bowl, then use a fork to mix in the cream. You want to create a paste similar in consistency to mashed potato.

Place the mushrooms on a baking tray and brush them all over with oil. Stuff with the cheese paste, then squash some small chunks of stale bread into the cheese. Top with some very thinly sliced leek, then brush the tops with a little more oil and sprinkle over some cracked black pepper. Bake in the oven for about 20 minutes, or until the tops start to brown and the mushrooms are cooked through. Serve with a handful of rocket.

Swap
Feel free to swap the Cheddar for whatever cheese you have in the fridge – and if you don't have leeks, spring onions will work well too.

POTATO & BROCCOLI FRITTATA

This is a bit like a Spanish omelette, but with a couple of shortcuts and a few extra ingredients. Frittatas are a great way to use up leftovers – you can swap the ingredients around depending on what you have in the fridge.

To make 1 portion

A few baby potatoes, halved

A few slices of onion

A few pieces of long-stem broccoli

3 eggs, beaten

Small handful of crumbled feta cheese

Olive oil

Salt and pepper

To cook

Preheat your oven to 180°C/gas mark 4.

Place the potatoes in a baking tray and drizzle with olive oil. Sprinkle over some salt, then place in the oven. After 10 minutes, add the onions to the tray and return to the oven. After another 10 minutes, add the broccoli and roast for 10 minutes more. Remove from the oven and set aside.

Add a splash of oil to a small non-stick frying pan over a medium heat. Add the eggs and season, then add the roasted potatoes, onions and broccoli. Cook for a few minutes, adding plenty of cracked black pepper. Cover the pan with a lid, baking tray or plate and cook for a few more minutes until the eggs are cooked through. Crumble over some feta cheese and serve.

PEANUT BUTTER CURRY

That's right: peanut butter isn't just for sandwiches. It's actually the key ingredient in some curries too. This recipe is a great way to use up the bits from an old jar.

To make 1 portion

½ mug basmati rice

1 mug water

½ aubergine, chopped into big chunks

Splash of sesame oil

1 garlic clove, grated

2cm piece of fresh root ginger, grated

1 tsp curry powder

1 tbsp peanut butter

200g coconut milk (from a 400g tin)

A few coriander leaves (optional)

A few slices of red chilli (optional)

Salt and pepper

To cook

Put the rice and the water in a saucepan with a pinch of salt. Cover with a lid and place over a medium heat for about 7 minutes until all the water is absorbed and the rice is cooked.

Meanwhile, fry the aubergine in a dry pan over a medium heat for about 8 minutes, then add the sesame oil, garlic, ginger, curry powder and peanut butter. Continue to cook for a few minutes more, then add the coconut milk and simmer for about 10 minutes until it's nice and thick. Season to taste, then serve with the rice, garnished with a few coriander leaves and chilli slices.

Tip

You can use up the rest of the coconut milk in another curry recipe – try the Thai Pea Curry on page 106 or the Coconut Chickpea Curry on page 198.

SPRING ONION NOODLES

Spring onions are the most important part of any noodle dish: they provide that all-important depth of flavour. So, how about a noodle dish with triple the spring onions?! This is a great dish to whip up for a quick meal, and most of the ingredients will already be in your storecupboard.

To make 1 portion

6 spring onions

1 garlic clove, crushed

1 red chilli (or a pinch of chilli flakes), sliced

1 nest of your favourite kind of noodles

Sprinkle of gravy granules (or ⅛ stock cube, crumbled)

Splash of soy sauce

Sesame oil

Salt

To cook

Chop your spring onions randomly so the pieces are different sizes. Season with salt and pepper, then pan-fry, along with the garlic and chilli, in a splash of olive oil over a medium heat for a few minutes.

Meanwhile, cook the noodles in a pan of boiling water according to the packet instructions. Once cooked, use tongs to transfer the noodles to the frying pan containing the spring onions, garlic and chilli (you want the noodles to still be a bit wet). Sprinkle over the gravy granules and a splash of soy sauce, then mix well and serve.

Tip
This is the perfect dish for using up any veggie scraps you have kicking around in the fridge – just fry them up with the spring onions and enjoy.

ROOT VEG PEEL CRISPS

This is a great way of using up vegetable peelings, although if you prefer you can just grab a piece of veg and turn the whole thing into strips with a peeler. Here, I have used beetroot, parsnip and carrot.

To make 1 portion

Handful of root vegetable peelings (beetroot, parsnip, carrot)

Salt

Vegetable oil

To cook

Either heat a few inches of oil in a deep pan over a medium–high heat, or get out your deep-fat fryer and set it to a medium–heat high heat (180°C). Once the oil is hot, drop the veg peelings into the oil and cook for about 5–10 minutes, removing with a slotted spoon once they are nice and crisp. Place on a plate lined with kitchen towel to drain, and sprinkle with salt. Serve straight away.

Tip

To see if the oil is hot enough to begin frying, just drop a small piece of vegetable peel into the pan and see if it sizzles.

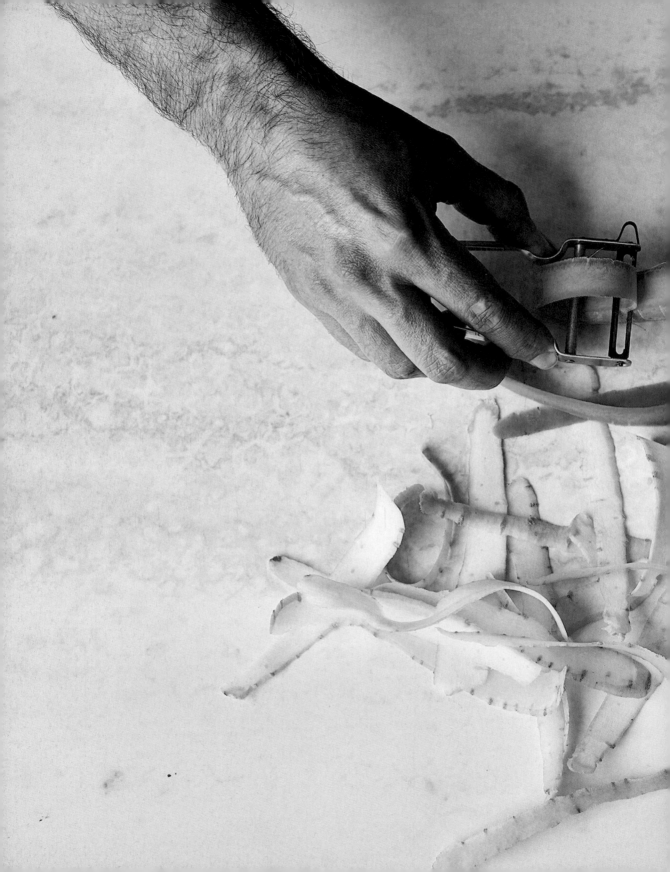

BURRATA POMODORO

Burrata is expensive, so if you can't find it for a decent price, this recipe works equally well with normal mozzarella. Just half a ball of this mild and creamy cheese will elevate an extremely simple tomato pasta into something far more extravagant and impressive (when really all you've done is put some cheese on it).

To make 1 portion

125g spaghetti

A few cherry tomatoes, halved (optional)

1 garlic clove, crushed

200g chopped tomatoes (from a 400g tin)

Pinch of dried oregano

Fresh basil leaves, to serve (optional)

½ ball burrata or mozzarella cheese

Olive oil

Salt and pepper

To cook

Cook the spaghetti in a pan of salted boiling water according to the packet instructions. Once cooked, drain and save a little of the pasta water.

Pan-fry the cherry tomatoes in a generous glug of olive oil over a medium–high heat for a few minutes, then add the garlic and continue to fry for a few more minutes. Next add the chopped tomatoes, then season with salt, pepper and oregano and cook for about 5 minutes more.

Mix the cooked spaghetti into the sauce, along with a drizzle of olive oil and a splash of pasta water. Transfer to a bowl and serve topped with burrata and some cracked black pepper, plus a couple of fresh basil leaves (if using).

> ### Tip
> Use the other half of the tinned tomatoes for the Aubergine Parm Burger on page 64.

MOZZARELLA-STUFFED CABBAGE

This is a great way of using up cabbage leaves: classic Italian flavours all wrapped in leaves and served in a simple tomato sauce. These oozy cheese parcels aren't traditional, but they are delicious.

To make 1 portion

3 savoy cabbage leaves

½ ball mozzarella cheese, cut into 3 pieces

4 pinches of dried oregano

½ onion, sliced

1 garlic clove, crushed

200g chopped tomatoes (from a 400g tin)

Olive oil

Salt and pepper

To cook

Preheat the oven to 180°C/gas mark 4.

Place the cabbage leaves in a bowl of freshly boiled water for 10 minutes to soften, then drain. Wrap a piece of mozzarella in each leaf, along with a pinch of oregano and some salt and pepper.

Next, grab a casserole dish and use it to fry the onion in a generous glug of olive oil over a medium heat. After a few minutes, add the crushed garlic and continue to fry for a further minute or two. Add the chopped tomatoes and the final pinch of oregano, then season with salt and pepper and simmer for 5 minutes.

Add the cabbage parcels to the tomato sauce and transfer to the oven for 15 minutes. Drizzle with olive oil and serve.

Tip

These cabbage parcels can be a creative way of using up various leftovers – just wrap them up in the cabbage leaves instead of the mozzarella.

GNOCCHI POMODORO

This recipe is all about using up that leftover cheese in the fridge: the more the better, and don't be afraid of mixing. Here I've added a bit of Stilton along with a little Cheddar, for a dramatic depth of flavour.

To make 1 portion

200g chopped tomatoes (from a 400g tin)

Handful of shop-bought gnocchi

Handful of grated Cheddar cheese

A few small chunks of stilton

1 tsp dried oregano

Olive oil

Salt and pepper

To cook

Preheat your oven to 180°C/gas mark 4.

Grab an ovenproof dish and add the chopped tomatoes and gnocchi. Add some of the grated cheddar and chunks of Stilton, then season with salt, pepper and oregano. Give it a little stir, then scatter over the rest of the cheese and drizzle with olive oil. Bake for about 35 minutes and serve.

Swap
You can use whatever kind of cheese you like.

HERB STEM FRITTERS

Ever wondered what to do with all those leftover herb stems? It's easy – stick them into a fritter. Each batch is a total surprise: just use whatever herb stalks you've got.

To make 1 portion

2 spring onions, sliced

Small handful of frozen peas, defrosted

1 egg, beaten

2 tbsp plain flour

Handful of any leftover cheese (such as Cheddar, Brie or feta), grated, crumbled or finely diced

Handful of leftover herb stalks, finely chopped

Olive oil

Salt and pepper

To cook

In a bowl, mix together the spring onions, peas, egg, flour, cheese and herb stalks. Season with salt and pepper. Place a frying pan over a medium heat and add a splash of olive oil, then use a big serving spoon to add about a quarter of the mixture to the pan in one big dollop. Repeat until you have 4 fritters. Fry them for about 5 minutes on each side, then serve.

TIKKA HALLOUMI

I like the tasty charred bits you get on chicken tikka cooked in a tandoor oven, but it's actually quite difficult to achieve this effect with normal home appliances. So, I tried recreating it with halloumi instead, as it's cheese that takes on colour well. It worked brilliantly, so now you can make your own perfectly charred tikka – and there's no need for chicken, so it's meat-free.

To make 1 portion

½ mug rice

1 mug water

Pinch of ground turmeric

A few slices of halloumi

1 tsp curry powder

Shop-bought crispy fried onions (or fry your own)

Handful of chopped coriander

Olive oil

Salt

To cook

Put the rice, water and turmeric in a saucepan with a pinch of salt. Cover with a lid and place over a medium heat for about 7 minutes until all the water is absorbed and the rice is cooked.

Meanwhile coat the halloumi in oil and curry powder, then pan-fry over a medium heat for a few minutes on each side until nicely charred.

Serve with the rice and garnish with crispy fried onions and coriander.

CHORIZO & ROASTED RED PEPPER ORECCHIETTE

Don't worry if you can't be bothered to blend the red peppers: just chop them small and it'll be fine, trust me. The important thing is to make sure you put the oil in: that's the key to this recipe.

To make 1 portion

Handful of dried orecchiette pasta

A few slices of roasted red pepper from a jar, plus a big splash of the oil

Handful of cooking chorizo, sliced

Salt and pepper

To cook

Cook the orecchiette in a pan of boiling salted water according to the packet instructions. Once cooked, drain and save a little of the pasta water.

Pop the roasted red pepper slices in a blender, along with a big splash of oil from the jar, and blend until smooth.

Meanwhile, pan-fry the chorizo for a few minutes over a medium heat until it starts to char and its paprika-infused oils are released. Then add the blended red peppers, the orecchiette and a splash of the reserved pasta water. Stir to combine and cook for a couple more minutes, then season and serve.

CURRIED SQUASH TURNOVER

The perfect packed lunch: a beautiful, soft and gooey curried squash filling, surrounded by a crispy, flaky pastry crust.

To make 1 portion (2 turnovers)

A few cubes of peeled and chopped butternut squash

½ onion, sliced

1 tsp curry powder

2 squares of puff pastry, approximately 10cm x 10cm

1 egg, beaten (optional)

Olive oil

Salt and pepper

To cook

Preheat your oven to 180°C/gas mark 4.

Place the squash cubes on a baking tray. Drizzle with olive oil, then sprinkle with salt, black pepper and the curry powder. Roast for about 30 minutes, adding the onions halfway through. Remove from the oven (leave the oven on) and allow to cool a little, then crush very slightly with a fork.

Line a clean baking tray with greaseproof paper and place the pastry squares on the lined tray. Spoon half of the filling into the middle of each square, then fold in half diagonally and gently seal the edges of the pastry by applying light pressure with your fingertips or the back of a fork.

Brush with egg, if you wish, then bake for about 20 minutes or until golden brown.

Enjoy straight away or allow to cool and take them with you as a packed lunch – these are just as delicious cold.

Swap

If you don't want to use an egg wash, brush the turnovers with a little oat milk before baking for a plant-based alternative.

GREEN MAC & CHEESE

Go green with your mac and cheese and sneak those veggies in! Here's an easy way to do it using frozen spinach. There's no extra cooking required: it just defrosts in the pan straight from the freezer. I've even added some green to the crispy breadcrumb topping.

To make 1 portion

Handful of macaroni

1 tsp butter

1 tsp plain flour

200ml milk

3 discs of frozen spinach

Handful of grated Cheddar cheese

Handful of breadcrumbs (see Tip)

Handful of finely chopped parsley

1 garlic clove, crushed

Olive oil

Salt and pepper

To cook

Cook the macaroni in a pan of boiling salted water according to the packet instructions. Once cooked, drain, then drizzle with olive oil and set aside until needed.

Meanwhile, melt the butter in a saucepan over a medium heat. Stir in the flour and cook for a few minutes, then add the milk, a little at a time, stirring continuously. Once the mixture has formed a sauce, add the frozen spinach and stir until defrosted. Remove from the heat and add the cheese, stirring until it melts into the sauce. Now stir in the drained pasta, then season to taste and transfer to an ovenproof dish (you can stir in an extra splash of milk if it needs loosening).

In a small bowl, mix together the breadcrumbs, parsley and crushed garlic, and season with a pinch of salt and pepper. Add a glug of olive oil, then sprinkle the breadcrumb mixture over the mac and cheese. Bake for about 15 minutes, or until the breadcrumbs are nicely toasted, then serve.

Tip

Making breadcrumbs is a great way to use up stale bread: simply take a slice or two of stale bread and grate it or whizz it up in a food processor. Any extra can be frozen.

BLACK OLIVE PESTO WITH SPAGHETTI

Pesto is expensive because it contains premium ingredients, so here is an easy alternative using a jar of black olives. These are great because they are packed with a powerful and distinct flavour.

To make 1 portion

125g spaghetti

Handful of black olives, plus a few extra, halved, to garnish

Handful of rocket

Small handful of grated Parmesan, plus extra to serve

Olive oil

Salt and pepper

To cook

Cook the spaghetti in a pan of salted boiling water according to the packet instructions, then drain.

Meanwhile, place the olives, rocket and Parmesan in a food processor, along with a big glug of olive oil, and blitz to make a paste. Loosen with loads more olive oil and season to taste.

Mix the cooked pasta with the black olive pesto, then serve, garnished with a little more Parmesan, some halved black olives, an extra drizzle of olive oil and some cracked black pepper.

Tip

This black olive pesto is also great on toast as a tapenade. You could also stir it into soup or drizzle it over fried eggs.

PULLED CHICKEN & BLACK BEAN CHILLI

Replacing beef with chicken is a small step in the right direction when it comes to reducing your impact on the environment. Why not make a few small changes and get going in the right direction? This tasty chilli is great for a midweek meal.

To make 1 portion

1 chicken leg

½ red onion, sliced

1 garlic clove

1 tsp smoked paprika

1 tsp ground cumin

200g chopped tomatoes (from a 400g tin)

1 veg, chicken or beef stock cube

200g black beans (from a 400g tin), drained

Dollop of crème fraîche

A few coriander leaves (optional)

A few slices of red chilli (optional)

Olive oil

Salt and pepper

To cook

Season the chicken leg and place it in a saucepan or casserole dish with a splash of olive oil over a medium heat. Add the onion and cook for about 10 minutes until the chicken is coloured on all sides. Next add the garlic, paprika and cumin, and continue to fry for a couple more minutes before adding the chopped tomatoes and the stock cube. Stir to combine, then cover with a lid and simmer for about 25 minutes, adding a splash of water if required.

Remove the chicken from the sauce and place on a plate. Use a fork to shred the meat. Discard the bone and return the meat to the saucepan. Add the black beans to the pan and simmer for another couple of minutes.

Season to taste and serve with a dollop of crème fraîche, and a few coriander leaves and slices of chilli to garnish.

Tip

For a veggie option, just leave out the chicken and chuck in some extra veg or more black beans.

GRIDDLED SQUARE POLENTA MEATBALLS

OK, so they're not made of meat, and they're not balls – but they are delicious. I could have tried to make them round, but this version is easier (and more fun).

To make 1 portion

½ mug of polenta

2 mugs of water

1 vegetable stock cube

2 pinches of dried oregano

½ onion, finely diced

2 garlic cloves, crushed or grated

200g chopped tomatoes (from a 400g tin)

Handful of fresh spinach

Handful of grated Parmesan cheese

Olive oil

Salt and pepper

To cook

Put the polenta and water in a small saucepan over a medium heat, along with the stock cube and a pinch of the oregano. Season with a pinch of salt and pepper and stir continuously for about 10 minutes until thick. Pour into a square container (you want the polenta to be about 3cm thick) and leave to set and cool for an hour or so.

Once set, cut the polenta into 3cm cubes, then transfer to a griddle pan. Drizzle with a tiny bit of olive oil and griddle over a medium–high heat for a few minutes on each side to create nice char marks and warm through.

Meanwhile, pan-fry the diced onions in plenty of olive oil over a medium heat for about 4 minutes, then add the garlic. Continue to fry for a couple more minutes, then add the chopped tomatoes and a splash of water. Season with salt, pepper and another pinch of oregano, then simmer for about 10 minutes, adding a handful of spinach for the final 30 seconds.

Mix the polenta squares with the sauce, then garnish with Parmesan and serve.

AUBERGINE PARM BURGER

You probably already know that aubergine parmigiana is amazing, especially when it's topped with crispy breadcrumbs. I was trying to come up with a way of completely covering the aubergine with breadcrumbs (without it going soggy) – and the aubergine parm burger was born.

To make 1 portion

1 tbsp plain flour

1 egg, beaten

Handful of breadcrumbs (see Tip)

2 x 1.5cm slices of aubergine

200g chopped tomatoes (from a 400g tin)

Pinch of dried oregano

2 thin slices of mozzarella cheese

1 bread roll

Handful of rocket, to garnish

Olive oil

Salt and pepper

To cook

Put the flour in one bowl, the beaten egg in another, and the breadcrumbs in a third. Season the flour and breadcrumbs with salt and pepper. Grab your aubergine slices and dust in the seasoned flour, then dip in the beaten egg and finally in the seasoned breadcrumbs. Shallow-fry in a generous glug of oil over a low–medium heat for about 5 minutes on each side, or until golden brown and cooked through. Place some mozzarella on each aubergine slice. Preheat the grill to medium, then transfer the cheesy aubergine slices to the grill for a minute or so until the mozzarella melts.

In the same pan you used for the aubergine, mix together the chopped tomatoes and oregano and season with salt and pepper. Simmer over a medium heat for about 5 minutes until thick.

Assemble the layers of aubergine, mozzarella and tomato sauce in the bread roll to create a burger. Top with a little rocket then serve.

Tip

To make the breadcrumbs, simply whizz up some stale bread in a food processor. It's a great way of using up bread that's a few days old.

GNOCCHI SOUP

Dumplings are a great addition to soups, so why not gnocchi? I know it sounds strange, but it really does work brilliantly. If you don't want to blend the soup, just chop the onion extra small and make a chunkier, more rustic version.

To make 1 portion

½ onion, diced

1 garlic clove, diced

200g chopped tomatoes (from a 400g tin)

200ml water

½ vegetable stock cube

Handful of shop-bought gnocchi

Splash of single cream

Basil leaves, to serve (optional)

Olive oil

Salt and pepper

To cook

Pan-fry the onions in a splash of olive oil over a medium–low heat for about 7 minutes, seasoning with salt and pepper. Add the garlic and continue to fry for a few more minutes. Next, add the chopped tomatoes and water, and crumble in the stock cube. Simmer for about 10 minutes, adding an extra splash of water if it looks too thick. If it looks too watery, just simmer for a little longer.

Transfer the soup to a blender (or use a stick blender) and blend until smooth. Return to the pan, then add the gnocchi and simmer for another 3–5 minutes until the gnocchi is cooked through. Serve with a splash of cream and a few basil leaves, if you like.

Tip
You can use up the rest of the chopped tomatoes and gnocchi in my Gnocchi Pomodoro on page 46.

CAULIFLOWER & BASIL KRAPOW

Technically, krapow should be made with a special kind of basil called Thai basil, but it's not that easy to get hold of. So here, I just use the regular kind of basil that you put on pizzas or serve with pasta. It still tastes great and means you can whip this up in no time using basic ingredients.

To make 1 portion

½ mug basmati rice

1 mug water

¼ head of cauliflower, cut into florets

1 shallot, sliced into thin circles

1 garlic clove, grated or crushed

1 chilli, sliced

2 tbsp honey

2 tbsp soy sauce

Handful of basil

Splash of sesame oil

Olive oil

Salt and pepper

To cook

Put the rice and the water in a saucepan with a pinch of salt. Cover with a lid and place over a medium heat for about 7 minutes until all the water is absorbed and the rice is cooked.

Meanwhile, season the cauliflower and pan-fry in a splash of oil over a high heat for a few minutes until it softens a bit and has a nice colour. Then add the shallot, garlic and chilli, and continue to fry for a further few minutes. Next add the honey, soy sauce and a splash of sesame oil. Keep stirring and basting so everything is lovely and sticky. Finally stir in the basil and, once it has wilted, serve with the rice.

> **Tip**
> Stir in some of the cauliflower leaves too to reduce food waste and add some greenery.

AUBERGINE 'BACON', PEA & LEMON CARBONARA

Lighten up your carbonara with some peas and a squeeze of lemon to bring some vibrancy and freshness to a traditionally heavy dish. I've also used aubergine and a pinch of paprika to create a veggie bacon alternative, making this meat-free but every bit as tasty.

To make 1 portion

Handful of pasta shells

Handful of frozen peas

¼ aubergine, diced into 1cm cubes

Pinch of smoked paprika

2 egg yolks

Squeeze of lemon and a little grated zest

Small handful of grated Parmesan cheese

Olive oil

Salt and pepper

To cook

Cook the pasta in a pan of salted boiling water according to the packet instructions, adding the peas a few minutes before the end. Once cooked, drain and save a little of the pasta water.

Meanwhile, drizzle the aubergine squares with olive oil and sprinkle over the smoked paprika. Fry in a dry frying pan over a medium heat for about 10 minutes until dark in colour.

In a bowl, mix together the egg yolks and most of the Parmesan (keeping some back for garnish). Add lots of cracked black pepper, along with some grated lemon zest and a squeeze of juice.

Add the cooked pasta and peas to the egg bowl, along with a splash of pasta water. Stir to combine, then mix in the aubergine. Serve topped with the remaining Parmesan and some more cracked black pepper.

Tip

This aubergine bacon is a game changer, so use it wherever you can. It's great in quiches and omelettes, and makes a brilliant pizza topping too.

VEG PEEL PAKORAS

Here's an idea for using up those vegetable peelings. Instead of throwing them away, why not have a go at making these tasty zero-waste pakoras? You can use any veg you like. Here, I used some carrot and potato peelings because that's what I had left over. I even chucked in some old coriander, but that is totally optional.

To make 1 portion

Handful of vegetable peelings (I used carrot and potato)

Handful of coriander (it doesn't matter if it's past its best)

3 tbsp chickpea flour

1 tsp curry powder

Splash of water

Vegetable oil

Salt and pepper

To cook

Either heat a few inches of oil in a deep frying pan over a medium heat, or get out your deep-fat fryer and set it to a medium heat (around 170°C).

In a bowl, mix together the vegetable peelings, coriander, flour, curry powder and a pinch of salt and pepper. Add a little water, a splash at a time, until you get a batter-like consistency. It should look as if you have coated the veg in a few tablespoons of yogurt.

Drop the mixture into the hot oil, adding 1 table-spoon at a time, and fry for about 3 minutes until golden brown.

Set aside on a plate lined with paper towels to drain while you cook the remaining pakoras, then serve.

Tip
To see if the oil is hot enough for you to begin frying, drop a small blob of batter into the pan. If it sizzles in the oil, you can start frying.

PIL PIL PASTA

In Spain, we dunk bread into a delicious chilli- and garlic-infused oil, so I thought maybe a pasta dish using this philosophy would work nicely too. Pasta can be delicious simply dressed in olive oil, but the addition here of chilli, garlic and prawns is amazing.

To make 1 portion

150g linguine

1 garlic clove, sliced

Pinch of cayenne pepper or chilli powder

Pinch of dried chilli flakes or fresh sliced chilli

Handful of prawns, peeled (cooked or uncooked)

Pinch of chopped parsley

Olive oil

To cook

Cook the pasta in a pan of salted boiling water according to the packet instructions. Once cooked, drain and set aside.

Meanwhile, add a huge glug of olive oil to a cold frying pan. Add the garlic, then place over a medium heat and fry gently for a couple of minutes to infuse the oil with flavour, but not long enough to colour the garlic. Next add the cayenne pepper or chilli powder, along with the chilli flakes or fresh chilli. Stir, then add the prawns and fry for a couple more minutes.

Mix the pasta with the garlic and chilli oil and prawns, then garnish with the chopped parsley and serve.

CHICKEN DRUMSTICK CASSOULET

One of my favourite complete meals in a pot has to be cassoulet: you get the carb element from the beans, a lovely rich sauce and whatever you choose as the hero ingredient. Here I have gone for chicken drumsticks, which are affordable and delicious.

To make 1 portion

2 chicken drumsticks, skin on

½ red onion, sliced

200g cannellini beans (from a 400g tin), drained

Pinch of dried oregano

200g chopped tomatoes (from a 400g tin)

½ vegetable stock cube

Olive oil

Salt and pepper

To cook

Season the chicken drumsticks with salt and pepper, then pan-fry in a splash of olive oil over a medium heat for about 10 minutes, turning occasionally to colour all sides.

Add the onion and continue to fry for a further 5 minutes. Add the cannellini beans, oregano and chopped tomatoes, then crumble in the stock cube and season. Simmer for about 10 minutes, then serve.

Swap
If you don't have cannellini beans, swap them for canned chickpeas.

CABBAGE RIBBON STIR-FRY

Sneak some extra greens into your meal with this simple and healthy swap from noodles to cabbage. Just cut it into strips and it'll do a similar job – and you don't need to boil the ribbons first, so that's some washing-up saved, too. Here I've used one of my favourite dipping sauces as a sauce for the ribbons.

To make 1 portion

⅛ white cabbage, cut into strips

½ red onion, cut into wedges

1 carrot, cut into matchsticks

1 spring onion, roughly chopped

1 garlic clove, sliced

1 tbsp Chinese crispy chilli sauce in oil, plus 1 tsp to garnish

Sesame oil

Salt and pepper

To cook

Season the cabbage strips with salt and pepper, then pan-fry in a splash of sesame oil and a splash of water over a medium heat for a few minutes until softened. Add the red onion, carrot, spring onion and garlic, and continue to pan-fry for a few more minutes. Stir in the crispy chilli sauce, then serve with extra sauce to garnish.

GENERAL TSO'S TOFU

This is a hugely popular dish in America, and no doubt it'll catch on soon in the UK. It's usually made with chicken, but here I have adapted it slightly to create a delicious and more sustainable tofu version.

To make 1 portion

Handful of cubed tofu

1 tbsp plain flour

1 garlic clove, sliced

2 spring onions, finely sliced

2 tbsp tomato ketchup

Splash of soy sauce

Pinch of dried chilli flakes

Pinch of sesame seeds

Sesame oil

Salt and pepper

To cook

Dust the tofu in the flour and a pinch of salt and pepper, then pan-fry in a splash of sesame oil over a medium–high heat for about 4 minutes on each side until golden brown. Add the garlic and spring onions and continue to cook. After a couple of minutes, when the garlic starts to brown, add the ketchup, soy sauce and chilli flakes, along with another splash of sesame oil. This will create the sauce. Simmer down for about 1 minute until sticky, then serve, garnished with sesame seeds.

SMASH BURGERS

Now, I'm not suggesting you can't eat meat at all. Why not just think about making it more of a treat? And you don't have to eat out to get a decent burger. You can make great burgers at home – just give these a chance, and you'll see. The secret is to do them exactly like this. Add nothing to the meat – just grab a small handful from the packet and chuck it in the pan, then sprinkle with some salt, squash it down and get it really caramelised. That's where the flavour comes from. So, next time you're craving a really good burger, save yourself the journey and expense and make your own.

To make 1 portion

2 small handfuls of minced beef

Small handful of grated Cheddar

Burger bun, toasted

Mustard

Ketchup

Salad (lettuce, onion, tomato)

Salt

To cook

Preheat your frying pan over a medium–high heat. Take your 2 handfuls of beef mince and roll each one into a golf-ball-sized ball. Drop them into the pan (you don't need any oil here) and squash them down using something flat, like a fish slice, then season with salt. Fry for a few minutes until charred, then flip them over to cook on the other side, placing some grated Cheddar on top of each one. After a few more minutes, when the burger is cooked through and nicely charred and the cheese is melting, add the burgers to a toasted bun. Top with your choice of mustard, ketchup, and whatever salad you have.

Tip

Serve with the Spicy Potato Peel Chips on page 144.

LEEK & MUSHROOM BARLEY RISOTTO

Leeks and mushrooms are a robust flavour combination that you can always count on: nothing can go wrong when you're combining these two. It's guaranteed to be delicious.

To make 1 portion

½ onion, diced

Handful of pearl barley

½ vegetable stock cube

300ml water

½ leek, sliced

Handful of mushrooms, sliced

1 thyme sprig

Small handful of grated Parmesan cheese, plus a few shavings for garnish

Olive oil

Salt and pepper

To cook

Pan-fry the onion in a splash of olive oil over a medium heat for about 10 minutes until soft, then add the barley and cook for a further minute. Crumble in the ½ stock cube and pour over the water. Simmer for about 15–20 minutes until the barley is cooked but still retains a slight bite, adding more water if needed.

Meanwhile, pan-fry the leek and mushrooms in a splash of olive oil over a medium heat for about 12 minutes until soft, adding the thyme halfway through.

Stir some grated Parmesan into the barley risotto, then add the leek and mushrooms. Season to taste, and serve with a few shavings of Parmesan to garnish.

Swap

To make this vegetarian/vegan, omit the Parmesan cheese. If you like, you can replace it with a sprinkling of nutritional yeast.

ONE-POT FETA & CHERRY TOMATO ORZO

I wanted to make an even easier version of that pasta dish that went viral on TikTok, so instead of cooking the pasta separately, I just used orzo and threw it in the same dish.

To make 1 portion

100g feta cheese

Handful of cherry tomatoes

Handful of orzo

Pinch of dried oregano

75ml water

Fresh basil leaves, to serve (optional)

Olive oil

Salt and pepper

To cook

Preheat your oven to 180°C/gas mark 4.

Put the feta, tomatoes and orzo in an ovenproof dish. Sprinkle over the oregano and season with salt and pepper, then add a couple of big glugs of olive oil and the water. Cook in the oven for about 20 minutes, checking halfway through to see if you need a splash more water. Give the orzo a quick stir at this point, but don't break up the tomatoes and feta too much.

Once it's cooked through, remove from the oven and give it another little stir to break up the feta and tomatoes. Scatter over some fresh basil leaves (if using), then serve.

TOMATO POKE BOWL

This is a great way to use up old tomatoes: just chop them into cubes and pretend they are sushi-grade tuna. Although it doesn't taste like tuna, this poke recipe works great with most things. The sauce and rice can elevate anything, transforming it into a beautiful lunchtime treat.

To make 1 portion

¼ mug rice

½ mug water

1 tbsp sesame oil

2 tbsp soy sauce

1 tsp rice wine vinegar

1 garlic clove, grated

1cm piece of fresh root ginger, grated

1 big tomato

½ carrot, cut into strips using a potato peeler

Small handful of shredded red cabbage

Small handful of edamame beans

Pinch of sesame seeds

Salt

To cook

Put the rice and the water in a saucepan with a pinch of salt. Cover with a lid and place over a medium heat for about 7 minutes until all the water is absorbed and the rice is cooked. Fluff with a fork to separate the grains.

Meanwhile, mix together the sesame oil, soy sauce, rice wine vinegar, garlic and ginger in a bowl, then add the chopped tomato.

Assemble the poke bowl by first adding the rice, followed by the carrot, cabbage, tomato and edamame beans. Pour the remaining marinade over the top and garnish with a pinch of sesame seeds.

Tip

This is great for packed lunches.

CHARRED LEEK WITH ROMESCO SAUCE

Romesco sauce sounds quite fancy, but it's really just a bit like a thick soup: all you need to do is roast some veg and blend it. This is a quick and easy sauce that looks pretty on the plate and will make anything seem more special.

To make 1 portion

1 leek, halved lengthways

1 red pepper, roughly chopped

1 large tomato, roughly chopped

1 garlic clove, peeled

½ tsp smoked paprika

Pinch of flaked almonds

Olive oil

Salt and pepper

To cook

Preheat your oven to 180°C/gas mark 4.

Place the leek on a baking tray. Drizzle with olive oil, season with salt and pepper, and roast for about 30 minutes.

Meanwhile, place the red pepper, tomato and garlic clove in an ovenproof dish. Season and drizzle with olive oil. Roast for about 15 minutes, then transfer to a blender. Add a splash of water and blend until smooth to create a romesco-style sauce.

Pour the sauce on to your plate in a pool, then place the charred leek on top and garnish with flaked almonds.

Swap

This romesco sauce is delicious with lots of other vegetables: try it over chargrilled long-stem broccoli or roasted asparagus.

GREEN HUMMUS

Sneak some extra veg into your hummus and create a striking vibrant green spread using my secret ingredient: frozen peas. Use a little extra of each ingredient as a garnish on top – it's always a nice touch.

To make 1 portion

2 slices of sourdough bread

200g chickpeas (from a 400g tin), plus extra for garnish

Handful of frozen peas, plus extra for garnish

2 spring onions, sliced, plus extra for garnish

Pinch of dried chilli flakes, plus extra for garnish

A few coriander leaves, to garnish (optional)

Olive oil

Salt and pepper

To cook

Drizzle the sourdough with olive oil and sprinkle over some salt, then toast under a hot grill or in a griddle pan over a medium heat.

Place the peas in a colander and hold under hot running water for a few minutes to defrost, then transfer to a food processor. Add the chickpeas, spring onions, chilli flakes, a generous glug of olive oil, and some salt and pepper, remembering to keep back the garnishes. Blitz to the consistency of hummus (adding more olive oil if necessary).

Spread the pea hummus on the toasted sourdough and top with the coriander, along with your reserved chickpeas, peas, spring onion slices and chilli flakes. Drizzle with olive oil, season with a pinch of salt and pepper and serve.

Tip

This hummus makes a great dip for the Courgette Koftas on page 128.

SUN-DRIED TOMATO PASTA

This pasta sauce requires no cooking, so it's the sort of recipe that will help you reclaim your evenings while still eating delicious food made from scratch.

To make 1 portion

½ jar sun-dried tomatoes in oil, plus the oil

A few sprigs of basil

Handful of grated Parmesan cheese

125g pasta of your choice

Olive oil

Salt and pepper

To cook

Cook the pasta in a pan of salted boiling water according to the packet instructions. Once cooked, drain and save a little of the pasta water.

Meanwhile, put the sun-dried tomatoes in a blender, along with the oil from the jar, the basil and the Parmesan. Blitz to form a smooth paste and season to taste.

Stir the paste into the cooked pasta, adding a splash of the pasta water to loosen. Serve immediately.

> **Tip**
> Feel free to mix and match your pasta shapes to use everything up.

GREEN LENTILS & CURRIED AUBERGINE

By oven-roasting veg with oil and curry powder, you get extra charring, and these chewy, slightly burned edges bring so much depth and flavour to the dish. For this to work, though, you need space. So don't let the veg overlap: that's the trick!

To make 1 portion

½ aubergine, sliced into long wedges

1 onion, half cut into wedges, half diced

2 tsp curry powder

1 carrot, diced

1 garlic clove, sliced

200g green lentils (from a 400g tin), plus half the liquid from the tin

Splash of single cream, plus extra to serve

Olive oil

Salt and pepper

To cook

Preheat your oven to 180°C/gas mark 4.

Put the aubergine and onion wedges in an ovenproof dish, making sure they don't overlap. Drizzle with a splash of olive oil, then sprinkle over 1 teaspoon of the curry powder and season with salt and pepper. Toss to coat, then roast for about 25 minutes until nicely coloured.

Meanwhile, pan-fry the diced onion and carrot in a splash of oil over a medium heat for about 3–4 minutes. Add the garlic and cook for another 3 minutes until it starts to colour, then add the green lentils, along with the reserved liquid from the tin. Stir in the remaining teaspoon of curry powder and a splash of cream, and season.

Transfer the lentils to a shallow bowl, and top with a pile of the charred aubergine and onion. Garnish with another splash of cream, and serve.

Tip

You can use up the rest of the lentils in my recipe for Cumin-spiced Lentils & Potatoes with Spinach & Yogurt (page 132).

EVEN EASIER FALAFEL

With every book I write, I spend a week getting obsessed with making falafel easier and easier, and now I think I've finally done it! Oven-roast the chickpeas for that falafel crunch, and chuck in the rest of the usual ingredients for that classic flavour.

To make 1 portion

100g chickpeas (from a 400g tin), drained

1 tsp ground cumin

Small handful of coriander, chopped

1 pitta bread, toasted

Salad (lettuce, onion and tomatoes)

Dollop of hummus

Olive oil

Salt and pepper

To cook

Preheat your oven to 180°C/gas mark 4.

Put the chickpeas in a baking tray, then drizzle with olive oil, season with salt and pepper, and sprinkle over the cumin. Roast for about 20 minutes until crispy, then remove from the oven and stir in the chopped coriander. Stuff into a toasted pitta bread with whatever salad you've got, plus a big dollop of hummus. Enjoy straight away.

Tip

If you have chickpeas left over, try making my Green Hummus on page 94, or the Coconut Chickpea Curry on page 198.

SAUTÉED BUTTER LEEKS WITH WILD RICE

Lately, I've really been enjoying the novelty of wild rice. Don't get me wrong, normal rice is perfectly fine: I just need an extra bit of excitement in my rice life to make me feel alive. Here, I've paired it with delicious buttery leeks.

To make 1 portion

½ mug of wild rice

½ leek, chopped into 1.5cm rounds

1 shallot, quartered

1 tsp Dijon mustard

1 tbsp butter

1 tbsp water

Salt and pepper

Olive oil

To cook

Cook the wild rice in a pan of water according to the packet instructions, until all the water is absorbed and the rice is cooked through.

Meanwhile, season the leek slices, then add them to a frying pan with the shallots and a glug of olive oil. Cook over a medium heat for 7 minutes, or until slightly coloured, then turn them over and cook for another 7 minutes, so they get coloured on both sides. Remove from the pan and set aside.

To make the sauce, keep the pan on the hob and increase the heat to high. Add the Dijon mustard, butter, water, and 1 tablespoon olive oil. Stir for a couple of minutes, then drizzle the sauce over the leeks and rice and serve.

Swap

If you prefer, you can swap the wild rice for regular rice.

THAI PEA CURRY

There are loads of curries that feature peas and potatoes, so I thought I'd mix together elements from a couple of different curries to create a new one. This is a quick and easy dinner, but it packs a healthy and tasty punch. You can add in any other veg you've got kicking around in the fridge, like carrots cut into matchsticks, diced peppers or a few broccoli florets.

To make 1 portion

½ mug of rice

1 mug of water

1 onion, sliced

A few small potatoes, halved

1 tbsp Thai green curry paste (see Tip)

200ml coconut milk (from a 400ml tin)

Handful of frozen peas

Handful of mangetout (optional)

1 red chilli, sliced, or a pinch of dried chilli flakes

Olive oil

Salt and pepper

To cook

Put the rice and the water in a saucepan with a lid and place over a medium heat. After about 7 minutes, when all the water is absorbed and the rice is cooked, turn off the heat and set aside.

Meanwhile, pan-fry the onion and potatoes in a splash of oil over a medium heat for about 10 minutes until they just start to colour. Add the Thai green curry paste and coconut milk and stir. Simmer for a few minutes, then add the peas and mangetout and simmer for a few minutes more until the vegetables are cooked. If the potatoes are taking a while and the sauce becomes too thick, just loosen with a splash of water. Season to taste, then garnish with sliced red chilli or dried chilli flakes and serve with the rice.

Tip

Some Thai curry pastes contain fish sauce, so remember to check the label if you're vegan or vegetarian.

CHICKEN SHAWARMA & BUTTER RICE

These kebabs are better when you make them in larger quantities, so here I've written the recipe to make enough for four people: that way, you can get a nice crispy coating, with succulent chicken in the middle.

To make 4 portions

8 chicken thighs, deboned, skin removed

1 tbsp ground cumin

1 tbsp paprika

1 tbsp dried oregano

1 mug of rice

2 mugs of water

A couple of red, orange or yellow peppers (I use the sweet pointed ones), sliced lengthways

Pinch of almond flakes

Knob of butter

Olive oil

Salt and pepper

To cook

Preheat your oven to 180°C/gas mark 4.

In a large bowl, mix the chicken with the cumin, paprika and oregano, along with a generous amount of salt, pepper and olive oil, ensuring the meat is evenly coated in the spices. Thread the chicken on to 2 skewers as shown and place on a baking tray. Roast for about 35 minutes until cooked through, adding the peppers to the tray halfway through the cooking time.

Meanwhile, make the rice. Put the rice and water in a saucepan with a lid and place over a medium heat. After about 7 minutes, when all the water is absorbed, turn off the heat, then add the butter and almond flakes. Set aside.

To serve, slice the meat off the kebab and serve with the rice and peppers.

GREEN BEANS & PESTO GNOCCHI

To make your pesto stretch further, you can 'water it down' by adding more olive oil. It's all about the ability to coat everything on the plate, and olive oil will help with that. Don't worry about diluting the flavour: trust me, you'll be able to taste the pesto just fine.

To make 1 portion

Handful of shop-bought gnocchi

Handful of green beans

2 tbsp pesto

Sprinkle of grated Parmesan cheese

Olive oil

Salt and pepper

To cook

Cook the gnocchi in a saucepan of salted boiling water according to the packet instructions. At the same time as you add the gnocchi to the saucepan, add the green beans too and cook together (the beans will take about 4 minutes to cook). Once cooked, drain.

Meanwhile, in a small bowl, mix the pesto with 2 tbsp olive oil. Stir this into the cooked gnocchi and beans. Garnish with lots of black pepper and a sprinkling of Parmesan, and serve.

ROASTED CHERRY TOMATO PAELLA

Stuck for an amazing meat substitute for paella? Spend a little time getting these cherry tomatoes to their absolute peak, and this will be a very special dish. I know supermarkets sell jars of sun-dried tomatoes, but what you actually want here are oven-roasted cherry tomatoes: these are the most delicious.

To make 1 portion

Handful of cherry tomatoes, halved

Pinch of dried oregano

½ onion, diced

1 garlic clove, sliced

50g paella or risotto rice

1 chicken or vegetable stock cube

200ml water

Pinch of saffron (optional)

Sprinkle of chopped parsley (optional)

Olive oil

Salt and pepper

To cook

Preheat your oven to 180°C/gas mark 4 and arrange half of the tomatoes in an ovenproof dish, cut-side up. Sprinkle with salt, pepper and oregano, then drizzle with olive oil. Roast for about 30 minutes or until the tomatoes are slightly charred around the edges.

Meanwhile, pan-fry the onion, the remaining tomatoes and the garlic in a big glug of olive oil over a medium heat. Season with salt and pepper. After about 10 minutes, stir in the rice. Continue to cook for a few more minutes, then add the stock cube, water and optional pinch of saffron. Reduce the heat to medium–low and simmer for about 20 minutes or until the water has been absorbed and the rice is cooked (add more water if needed, but do not stir: just let it bubble away without touching it).

Once the paella is cooked, add the oven-roasted cherry tomatoes, then garnish with parsley (if using) and serve.

AMERICAN CHOPPED SALAD

This is how Americans do salad. I thought it was a bit strange at first, but it actually does taste better – I'm not sure if it's psychological or if the flavours just mix better this way!

To make 1 portion

1 tbsp mayonnaise

1 tsp Dijon mustard

1 chicken thigh, deboned, skin removed

1 slice of bread, chopped into 1cm cubes

A few lettuce leaves, chopped into 1cm pieces

½ avocado, chopped into 1cm cubes

1 tomato, chopped into 1cm cubes

2 tbsp tinned sweetcorn

Olive oil

Salt and pepper

To cook

First, make the dressing by mixing the mayo and mustard with 3 tablespoons olive oil in a small bowl. Set aside.

Season the chicken with salt and pepper, then pan-fry in a splash of oil over a medium heat for about 7 minutes on each side until cooked through. Remove chicken from the pan (leaving the juices) and chop it into 1cm cubes.

Add the bread cubes to the same pan and fry over a medium heat for a few minutes until nicely golden and toasted.

Add the chopped lettuce, avocado and tomato to a bowl, along with the chicken, croutons and sweetcorn. Season to taste and drizzle with the dressing.

Swap

For a greener version, swap the avocado for chopped cucumber – and to make it veggie, why not swap the chicken for some leftover roasted sweet potatoes or squash?

STUFFED ROLLS

This is an unconventional and fun way to make a sandwich. Don't just cut open a bread roll lengthways and have one layer of flavour – go crazy and really increase that filling-to-bread ratio.

To make 1 portion

1 bread roll (any kind you like)

A few slices of mozzarella (or any bits of cheese you have in the fridge)

A few slices of roasted peppers from a jar

2 tbsp pesto

Fresh basil leaves, to serve (optional)

To cook

Preheat the oven to 180°C/gas mark 4.

Cut a series of slits in your bread, working your way down the length, but don't cut all the way through. Spread some pesto into each slit, then stuff with the peppers and mozzarella slices. Bake for about 5 minutes or until the cheese has melted, then serve with another dollop of pesto on top, plus a few basil leaves (if using).

Tip
This is delicious served warm and gooey, but it also makes a great treat to take along on a picnic or for a packed lunch.

PRAWNS & PEAS IN A TARRAGON SAUCE

This is a lovely summery dish with light flavours. Buying produce like asparagus in season is something I always look forward to, and combining it with frozen peas will help you reduce your overall waste: just grab a handful from the bag and stick it back in the freezer.

To make 1 portion

Handful of fresh or frozen peeled prawns

A few asparagus spears, roughly chopped

Handful of frozen peas

Big glug of single cream

Pinch of dried or fresh tarragon

Squeeze of lemon

Olive oil

Salt and pepper

To cook

Season the prawns with salt and pepper, then pan-fry them with the asparagus and peas in a splash of olive oil over a medium heat. After about 3–4 minutes, once the peas have defrosted and the asparagus is cooked, add the cream and tarragon. Simmer for another couple of minutes, then serve with a squeeze of lemon.

THE WHOLE SQUASH PASTA

This recipe uses the entire squash, even the skin and the seeds! They add a fantastic contrasting texture and are totally free – they come already included in the price of the squash, LOL.

To make 4 portions

1 butternut squash

450g pasta

A few sage leaves

Olive oil

Salt and pepper

To cook

Preheat your oven to 180°C/gas mark 4.

Peel your squash and chop it into 2cm cubes, keeping the seeds and peel to one side. Place the squash cubes on a baking tray and drizzle with olive oil. Season with plenty of salt and pepper, then roast for about 35 minutes.

Meanwhile, place the skins and seeds on a separate tray, spreading them out nicely. Drizzle with olive oil and season with salt and pepper, then put them in the oven for the final 15 minutes of the squash roasting time.

Meanwhile, cook the pasta in a pan of salted boiling water according to the packet instructions. Once cooked, drain and save a mugful of the pasta water.

Place the roasted butternut squash cubes in a blender, along with a big splash of the pasta cooking water and a generous glug of olive oil. Blend until smooth. Season to taste, then mix with the pasta. Serve topped with the sage leaves, crunchy squash seeds and crispy roasted squash skin.

GRATED HALLOUMI FAJITAS

If you grate halloumi, it goes so much further, giving you little crumbs of salty cheese that are perfect for these simple fajitas. Be sure not to add any salt: the halloumi is all you need here.

To make 1 portion

50g halloumi, grated

½ red onion, sliced

½ green pepper, sliced

Pinch of ground cumin

Pinch of paprika

A few tortillas

Dollop of crème fraîche

A few cherry tomatoes, quartered

Small handful of coriander (optional)

Pepper

Olive oil

To cook

Start by pan-frying the grated halloumi for a few minutes in a dry pan over a medium heat. Transfer to a plate and set aside, then return the pan to the heat and pan-fry the onion and green pepper in a splash of olive oil for 5 minutes. Season with pepper and sprinkle over the paprika and cumin – remember, there's no need for salt.

Gently heat the tortillas in a clean frying pan over a low heat, just to soften them up, then divide the onions and peppers between them. Top with the grated halloumi, then a little crème fraîche, a few tomato quarters and some coriander. Roll up and enjoy.

Tip

For something more substantial, add half a can of chickpeas or black beans to the pan when you're cooking the onion and pepper.

POTATOES, ASPARAGUS & PEAS WITH GARLIC BUTTER

I know it's just potatoes and veg, but this tastes way more exciting than it sounds. Keep the potato skins on: they are nutritious and add a rustic wholesomeness to this simple dish.

To make 1 portion

Handful of baby potatoes

2 tbsp butter

2 garlic cloves, crushed

A few asparagus spears

A small handful of frozen peas, defrosted

Small handful of chopped parsley

Handful of grated Parmesan cheese

Olive oil

Salt and pepper

To cook

Preheat your oven to 180°C/gas mark 4.

Place the potatoes on a baking tray, then drizzle with olive oil. Scatter over a pinch of salt, then roast for about 35 minutes until cooked through.

Once cooked, transfer the potatoes to a saucepan over a medium heat. Add the butter, garlic, asparagus and peas, then season. Once it starts to sizzle, cook for about 3 minutes, then serve topped with chopped parsley and grated Parmesan.

COURGETTE KOFTAS WITH RICE & TOMATO SALAD

I find Greek cuisine so fresh and vibrant – it's the perfect food to eat on a hot day. Here, I have come up with a great way to substitute meat for veg while keeping those great Greek flavours.

To make 1 portion (4 koftas)

¼ mug rice

½ mug water

½ courgette, grated

2 tbsp chickpea flour

Pinch of ground cumin

1 tomato, diced

¼ red onion, sliced

Squeeze of lemon juice

Olive oil

Salt and pepper

To cook

Put the rice and the water in a saucepan with a pinch of salt. Cover with a lid and place over a medium heat for about 7 minutes until all the water is absorbed and the rice is cooked. Set aside.

Place the grated courgette in a bowl and stir in the chickpea flour, along with a pinch of salt and the cumin. Leave for 5 minutes, then mix again.

Pan-fry dollops of the courgette mixture in a splash of olive oil over a medium heat, cooking for a few minutes on each side to create the koftas.

Meanwhile, make the tomato salad by mixing together the tomatoes and red onion in a small bowl. Drizzle over some olive oil and a squeeze of lemon. Season to taste, then leave to sit for 5 minutes to let the flavours mingle.

Serve the koftas with the rice and tomato salad.

HALLOUMI, AUBERGINE & TOMATO BAKE

Easy dinners are my speciality, making them look tasty with minimum effort. Halloumi goes a lovely golden brown in the oven and looks stunning here layered between slices of roasted aubergine. It's much easier than it looks. I've suggested you go for 4 servings here, as the dish makes a great centrepiece.

To make 4 portions

2 onions, sliced

4 garlic cloves, crushed or grated

400g tin chopped tomatoes

1 tsp dried oregano, plus an extra pinch

2 aubergines, sliced into 1cm thick slices

2 x 200g blocks of halloumi, sliced into 1cm thick slices

Olive oil

Salt and pepper

To cook

Preheat your oven to 180°C/gas mark 4.

Grab a casserole dish and use it to fry the onions in a splash of oil over a medium heat for about 5 minutes until nice and soft, adding the crushed garlic for the final minute. Add the chopped tomatoes and the 1 tsp oregano. Simmer for a few minutes and season to taste.

Arrange slices of aubergine and halloumi on top, alternating between the two, then drizzle with olive oil and sprinkle with an extra pinch of oregano.

Bake in the oven for about 25 minutes until slightly browned on top, then serve.

Swap

Courgettes and freshly sliced tomatoes also work brilliantly in this dish, so use what you have available.

CUMIN-SPICED LENTILS & POTATOES WITH SPINACH & YOGURT

Quick and easy, this makes a great lunchtime treat and is a fantastic way to use up any leftover potatoes without the hassle of having to boil them first: just chop them up small and cook it all in the same pan.

To make 1 portion

1 potato, diced, skin on

½ onion, sliced

½ tsp ground cumin

3 handfuls frozen spinach, defrosted

200g green lentils (from a 400g tin), drained

2 dollops of natural yogurt

Olive oil

Salt and pepper

To cook

Pan-fry the diced potato in a splash of olive oil over a medium heat for about 10 minutes until almost cooked, then add the onion and cumin and fry for a further 5 minutes. Next add the spinach. Season to taste, then add the lentils and a big dollop of yogurt. Cook for a few minutes more, then serve, garnished with another dollop of yogurt.

Swap

For a vegan version, swap the natural yogurt for coconut yogurt.

HONEY & MUSTARD CHICKPEAS WITH SWEET POTATO MASH

It's nice to balance the sweetness of honey with the bite of mustard to create a classic flavour combination. Slightly syrupy and delicious chickpeas all mopped up with a sweet potato mash.

To make 1 portion

1 large sweet potato

2 spring onions, roughly chopped

1 carrot, sliced

200g chickpeas (from a 400g tin), drained

2 tsp wholegrain mustard

1 tsp honey

100ml single cream

Olive oil

Salt and pepper

To cook

Preheat the oven to 180°C/gas mark 4 and roast the sweet potato for 40 minutes. Alternatively, pierce it several times with a fork and cook in the microwave on high for 6 minutes.

Meanwhile, pan-fry the spring onions and carrot in a splash of olive oil over a medium heat for a few minutes, then add the chickpeas, mustard, honey and cream. Stir and simmer for a few minutes until it thickens a little. Season to taste.

Using a tablespoon, scoop out the flesh of the sweet potato and mash it with a fork. Serve the mash with the honey and mustard chickpeas.

Swap

To make it vegan, swap the honey for maple syrup and use a plant-based cream.

Tip

Save the sweet potato skin and use it for loaded potato skins or stuff it like a taco for another meal.

CHARRED SWEETCORN & SALSA WITH BULGUR WHEAT

This one is all about that charred flavour you get from cooking a whole sweetcorn on the hob, so don't be afraid to get a little smoky. It's a great way of using sweetcorn straight from the farm, and is a perfect recipe for using up overripe tomatoes.

To make 1 portion

Handful of bulgur wheat

1 vegetable stock cube

1 sweetcorn cob

1 tomato, diced

2 spring onions, sliced

Squirt of sriracha sauce

1 tbsp crème fraîche

Pinch of smoked paprika

Olive oil

Salt and pepper

To cook

Place the bulgur wheat in a saucepan of boiling water and crumble in the stock cube. Cook for about 10 minutes until the bulgur wheat is cooked through, then drain.

Meanwhile, place the corn in a saucepan over a high heat and cook for a minute or two on each side to cook through and create some charring. Once cooked, carefully slice down the length of the corn cob to separate the sweetcorn kernels into strips.

In a small bowl, combine the tomato, spring onion and sriracha with a splash of olive oil to make a spicy salsa. Season to taste, then set to one side.

In a serving bowl, combine the charred sweetcorn and bulgur wheat. Add the salsa, then top with the crème fraîche and sprinkle over the smoked paprika.

PASTA ALLA NORMA

I had this at a restaurant called Norma and it was amazing! The humble aubergine is the star of this dish, which makes a delicious alternative to spaghetti bolognese. What better way to get more veg into your meal?

To make 1 portion

125g pasta of your choice

½ aubergine, roughly chopped

1 garlic clove, sliced

Pinch of dried chilli flakes

Pinch of dried oregano

200g chopped tomatoes (from a 400g tin)

Small handful of grated Parmesan cheese

Olive oil

Salt and pepper

To cook

Cook the pasta in a pan of salted boiling water according to the packet instructions. Once cooked, drain and save a little of the pasta water.

Meanwhile, pan-fry the chopped aubergine in a splash of olive oil over a medium heat for about 10 minutes. Add the garlic, oregano and chilli flakes, along with another splash of olive oil. Season with salt and pepper, then continue to cook for another few minutes until the garlic just starts to colour. Now add the chopped tomatoes and simmer for about 7 minutes.

Stir the cooked pasta into the sauce, adding a splash of the pasta water to loosen if needed. Serve with a scattering of Parmesan, a crack of black pepper and a little olive oil.

Tip

Use up the rest of the tinned tomatoes in one of my other recipes, like the Aubergine Parm Burger (page 64) or the Griddled Square Polenta Meatballs (page 62).

BROCCOLI & NOODLE SALAD WITH PEANUT DRESSING

I serve this dish at room temperature, but it is equally delicious served straight away, still hot, or even served cold as a packed lunch. Just make sure you don't overcook the broccoli stems – you want to keep some crunch.

To make 1 portion

1 nest of wholewheat noodles (check the packet if you're vegan)

A few pieces of long-stem broccoli

1 garlic clove, grated

4 tbsp soy sauce

juice of ½ lime

2 tbsp sesame oil

1 tbsp peanut butter (crunchy or smooth)

Sprinkle of sesame seeds, to garnish

To cook

Cook the noodles in a pan of boiling water according to the packet instructions. Cook the broccoli in the same pan at the same time until cooked but still firm – it will take about 5 minutes. Drain the broccoli and noodles and allow to cool a bit.

Meanwhile, make the sauce. In a bowl, mix together the garlic, soy sauce, lime juice, sesame oil and peanut butter. If the sauce is too thick, add a little water to thin it out.

Drizzle the sauce over the broccoli and noodles, then garnish with a sprinkle of sesame seeds.

SMASHED CUCUMBER SALAD

All too often, cucumber can be a bit boring, so you know a recipe that uses cucumber as the main ingredient has to be exceptional. The fresh, spicy flavours here make the simple ingredients more exciting.

To make 1 portion

½ cucumber

A few cherry tomatoes, halved

1 garlic clove, crushed or grated

1 red chilli, sliced

1 tsp crispy chilli oil

1 tsp rice wine vinegar

1 tsp sesame oil

1 tsp soy sauce

Salt

To cook

Lightly bash the cucumber with a heavy object like a rolling pin (this will increase its surface area and make it easier to get the excess liquid out), then slice the cucumber in half lengthways. Scrape out the seeds (see Tip), then slice the cucumber into 1cm thick slices, cutting at an angle. Place them in a bowl with a pinch of salt and leave to rest for 10 minutes, then discard any the liquid that comes out of the cucumber. Now add the tomatoes, garlic, chilli, crispy chilli oil, rice wine vinegar, sesame oil and soy sauce to the bowl. Mix to combine, then serve.

Tip
Try stirring the cucumber seeds into some yogurt with a little mint to make a tzatziki.

SPICY POTATO PEEL CHIPS

A huge amount of potato peelings are thrown away each week, so let's start using them up! Next time you're peeling potatoes for a Sunday roast, just take a little more care with your peeling to get bigger pieces, and save them for this chip recipe (the peelings will keep in the fridge for 1 day).

To make 1 portion

Handful of potato peelings

Pinch of paprika

Olive oil

Salt

To cook

Preheat your oven to 180°C/gas mark 4.

Spread out the potato peelings on a baking tray. Sprinkle with the paprika and some salt, and drizzle with olive oil. Cook in the oven for about 25 minutes, or until golden brown, giving the tray a shake halfway through. Serve with your favourite dip.

Swap
This recipe will also work for other peelings: try it with sweet potatoes or even carrots and parsnips.

SESAME PRAWN TOAST

It's fine to use cooked frozen prawns here: that's what I do, because that's what I have in my freezer. Also, it's difficult to save half an egg, so I usually double the quantities below to make 2 portions and save some for later.

To make 1 portion

Handful of defrosted cooked peeled prawns

1 spring onion, plus extra to serve

1 garlic clove

1 tsp soy sauce

½ egg, beaten

A few slices of any bread

Small handful of sesame seeds

½ carrot, cut into matchsticks

Small handful of lamb's lettuce (or any salad leaves)

Big dollop of sweet chilli sauce

Vegetable oil or sesame oil

Salt and pepper

To cook

Chuck the prawns, spring onion, garlic and soy sauce into a blender. Add the egg and blend to create a paste. Spread this paste over the bread.

Place the sesame seeds on a small plate, then dip each slice of the bread into the seeds.

Pan-fry the slices in a glug of oil over a medium heat for a minute or two on each side until golden brown. Serve with carrot matchsticks and salad leaves on the side, and a little bowl of sweet chilli sauce for dipping. Scatter over some sliced spring onion and enjoy.

HALLOUMI & COURGETTE KEBABS WITH A LEMON DRESSING

Kebabs are a fun and easy barbecue classic: just chop up the ingredients and stick them on a skewer. The clever part here is using ribbons of courgette so they cook quicker. I've also brushed these kebabs with a lemon and thyme marinade to infuse those flavours into the halloumi as it cooks.

To make 1 portion

A few cubes of halloumi

A few ribbons of courgette (see Tip)

juice of ¼ lemon

A few thyme sprigs

Salad (whatever you have)

Olive oil

To cook

Light a barbecue or preheat a griddle or frying pan over a medium heat.

Thread the halloumi cubes and courgette ribbons on to a skewer.

To make the marinade, mix together the lemon juice and a big glug of olive oil in a small bowl.

Place the skewer on the barbecue, griddle pan or frying pan and lightly brush on the marinade using the thyme sprig as a brush. Turn the skewer every couple of minutes until cooked on all sides. Enjoy with a salad, and add the thyme sprig brush to the serving dish as a garnish.

Tip

You can cut the courgette ribbons carefully with a knife, or simply use a potato peeler.

CAULIFLOWER LARB LETTUCE CUPS

A lovely summer dish, and easy to scale up to enjoy with friends: just place a big bowlful in the middle of the table and everyone can dig in and make their own lettuce wraps. Larb is usually made with meat, but here I've swapped it for tiny cauliflower florets for a veg-based version that's just as tasty.

To make 1 portion

½ red onion, finely diced

¼ head of cauliflower, chopped into small florets

1 garlic clove, grated or crushed

Pinch of dried chilli flakes

Pinch of curry powder

A few lettuce leaves

Handful of chopped coriander

½ lime

Olive oil

Salt and pepper

To cook

Season the onion and cauliflower, then pan-fry in a splash of olive oil over a medium heat for about 6 minutes. Add the garlic, chilli flakes and curry powder, and continue to fry for a few more minutes until everything is golden brown.

Spoon the mixture into lettuce leaves, then garnish with chopped coriander and squeeze over some lime before serving.

WATERMELON & FETA SALAD

Fresh and vibrant, this watermelon salad is perfect for when the weather gets hot and you need cooling down. There's no cooking required – just chuck everything in a bowl and serve.

To make 1 portion

1 slice of watermelon, chopped into cubes

A few chunks of feta cheese

¼ cucumber, roughly chopped

A few very thin slices of red onion

6 fresh mint leaves, 3 chopped and 3 left whole

Drizzle of balsamic glaze

Olive oil

Salt and pepper

To cook

Simply place the watermelon, feta, cucumber, onion and chopped mint in a bowl. Season and toss to combine, then dress with a drizzle of olive oil and the balsamic glaze. Serve topped with the whole mint leaves.

Tip

This is really easy to scale up to serve more people, so it's perfect for a summer barbecue. It also makes a great packed lunch on a hot day.

ROCKET & PARMESAN SOUP

An easy-peasy soup that has a nice peppery taste thanks to the rocket, and a savoury edge from the cheese. It's great for using up wilted rocket and those leftover ends of Parmesan.

To make1 portion

1 slice of stale bread

½ onion, diced

2 mugs of water

1 vegetable stock cube

Handful of rocket

Handful of grated Parmesan, plus a few shavings to garnish

Olive oil

Salt and pepper

To cook

Drizzle the bread with olive oil and sprinkle over some salt, then toast under a hot grill or in a griddle pan over a medium heat. Chop into squares and set aside.

Meanwhile, fry the onion in a splash of olive oil in a saucepan over a medium heat for about 5 minutes until it just starts to colour.

Chuck in the water, along with the stock cube, rocket and grated Parmesan. Bring to a simmer and let it bubble away for a couple of minutes. Transfer to a blender and blitz until smooth, then season to taste. Serve in a bowl with a garnish of shaved Parmesan and a drizzle of olive oil, with the croutons scattered over the top.

Tip

Add the Parmesan rind to the pan while cooking for extra flavour and scoop it out before you blend the soup.

BRAISED CHICKEN LEG

Don't lose those juices: that's the key to this dish. Just let the tomatoes pop and mix with the chicken juices and olive oil.

To make 1 portion

1 chicken leg, skin on

1 tsp oregano

Handful of cherry tomatoes

Handful of frozen peas

Olive oil

Salt and pepper

To cook

Preheat your oven to 180°C/gas mark 4.

Place your chicken leg in an ovenproof dish. Drizzle with plenty of olive oil and sprinkle with salt, black pepper and the oregano, then roast for about 30 minutes, or until cooked through. Add the tomatoes for the final 15 minutes, and the frozen peas about 5 minutes from the end, giving everything a good mix around so they are coated in the juices.

To serve, arrange the chicken leg on a plate and spoon over the tomatoes, peas and cooking juices.

Tip

Serve with a slice of bread for mopping up the juices.

VEGGIE SAUSAGE PASTA

A great swap for a greener meal is to replace regular sausages with veggie ones: they are packed with flavour. Here's an easy recipe for you to try. This is also a great recipe for using up those last bits of pasta in the packet – you can combine different shapes, so you never need to let any go to waste.

To make 1 portion

Big handful of any pasta

2 veggie sausages, sliced into 1cm slices

1 courgette, roughly chopped

1 tbsp red pesto

Olive oil

Salt and pepper

To cook

Cook the pasta in a pan of salted boiling water according to the packet instructions. Once cooked, drain and save a little of the pasta water.

Pan-fry the veggie sausages and courgette in a splash of olive oil over a medium heat for about 10 minutes until cooked through. Then add the pasta, along with the red pesto and a splash of cooking water. Season to taste and serve.

Swap

This will work well with most veg – try throwing in a handful of frozen peas if you don't have any courgette.

BANANA PEEL PULLED PORK BUN

I saw people cooking with banana peel on the internet and I was intrigued. Turns out it's actually quite delicious if you prepare it in the right way. Banana peel is definitely something I would usually throw away, so technically this is free food.

To make 1 portion

1 banana peel

½ tsp ground cumin

½ tsp smoked paprika

1 tsp demerara sugar (or other brown sugar)

3 tbsp tomato ketchup

1 soft bread roll

1 tbsp coleslaw

Olive oil

Salt

To cook

Shred the banana peel using a fork, then pan-fry in a splash of olive oil over a medium for about 5 minutes. Add a pinch of salt, along with the cumin, smoked paprika and sugar. After 30 seconds, add the ketchup and simmer for a couple more minutes until the mixture is the consistency and dark brown colour of pulled pork. Serve in a soft roll, topped with a tablespoon of coleslaw.

LEFTOVER BREAD PANZANELLA

This dish is perfect for using up leftover bread – in fact, you need it to be a little stale, or it will go too soggy. It's a tasty and satisfying summer dish.

To make 1 portion

A few slices of stale sourdough bread, torn into chunks

A few tomatoes, roughly chopped (any tomatoes will do)

1 red onion, sliced

1 tbsp balsamic vinegar

A few basil leaves, to garnish (optional)

Olive oil

Salt and pepper

To make

Place the chunks of stale bread in a bowl, along with the tomatoes and red onion. Add a generous pinch of salt and pepper, along with the balsamic vinegar and 5 tbsp olive oil. Mix it all together, then leave to stand for 5 minutes. Now give it another mix, garnish with a few basil leaves and serve.

Tip

I have to admit, sometimes I buy new bread just to make this recipe. If you decide to do the same, you just need to dry it out in the oven for a bit first.

CHICKEN & PEPPER TRAYBAKE

Oven-roasted peppers have a rich, sticky texture that perfectly complements the roasted chicken in this easy traybake recipe. If you like, you can add some chorizo, for an extra punch of flavour.

To make 1 portion

1 chicken thigh, skin on

Pinch of paprika

1 red pepper, roughly chopped or torn into big chunks

A few slices of cooking chorizo (optional)

Olive oil

To cook

Preheat your oven to 180°C/gas mark 4.

Rub the chicken with olive oil, salt, black pepper and paprika. Place on a baking tray and roast for about 30 minutes, adding the pepper and chorizo (if using) halfway through.

Serve drizzled with all those lovely paprika-infused juices left in the tray.

BROCCOLI STEM FRIED RICE

Here's an idea for using up those chunky broccoli stalks: just chop them up to create broccoli 'rice' and stir-fry.

To make 1 portion

½ head of broccoli

1 garlic clove, sliced

2 spring onions, each cut into about 5 pieces

¼ carrot, cut into matchsticks

1 fresh red chilli, sliced (or a pinch of dried chilli flakes)

Splash of soy sauce

Sesame oil

Salt and pepper

To cook

Chop the broccoli into florets and blitz in a food processor to form coarse chunks – they should be bigger than grains of rice. (If you don't have a food processor, you can chop the broccoli by hand with a knife or grate it.)

Pan-fry the garlic, spring onion, carrot and chilli in a splash of sesame oil over a high heat for a couple of minutes, or until the garlic just starts to colour. Add the chopped broccoli and continue to fry for 5–10 minutes, or until cooked. Season to taste, then transfer to a plate and add a splash of soy sauce before serving.

ZUCCHINI FRITTI

Yes, these fries are made from courgette, but I promise they are just as good as chips – and way posher. They're delicious paired with the lemon mayo dip. For the very best restaurant-quality *zucchini fritti*, you should salt the sliced courgette and leave it to drain to extract excess moisture before cooking. This isn't essential unless you're trying to impress someone, though, so feel free to skip that step if you want to.

To make 1 portion

1 courgette, sliced into thin French fries

4 tbsp plain flour

Pinch of paprika

Squeeze of lemon juice

2 tbsp mayo

Oil, for deep-frying

Salt and pepper

To cook

Place the sliced courgette fries in a colander and sprinkle with salt, then leave to rest for 20 minutes to extract excess moisture. Quickly rinse them, then pat dry with a paper towel. (As I said in the introduction, this step isn't essential, but will take your *fritti* to the next level.)

Meanwhile, heat your oil to about 180°C, either in a high-sided pan over a medium heat, or in a deep-fat fryer. To see if the oil is hot enough, drop in a small piece of courgette and see if it sizzles.

Put the flour in a bowl and season with a pinch of salt and a pinch of paprika. Dust the courgette pieces in the flour, then deep-fry in the hot oil for a few minutes until they start to colour. Work in very small batches to get the best crust, transferring the cooked *fritti* to a plate lined with paper towels while you cook the next batch.

Stir the lemon juice into the mayo in a small bowl, then serve alongside the *zucchini fritti*.

Tip
Sometimes you can get courgettes with flowers attached – this is actually the most sought-after part of the courgette, so don't chuck it away. Dust it in flour, then fry it along with the fritti.

GRILLED CAULIFLOWER CHEESE SANDWICH

Here's a twist on a grilled cheese sandwich: adding cauliflower. It makes for a decadent and filling sandwich, perfect when you are absolutely ravenous. Don't forget to use the cauliflower leaves – I promise they are delicious and should never be thrown away.

To make 1 sandwich

A few cauliflower florets, broken into small pieces, plus some leaves

1 tsp butter

1 tsp plain flour

100ml milk

Small handful of Cheddar cheese

2 slices of bread

Olive oil

Salt and pepper

To cook

Season the cauliflower florets and pan-fry in a splash of olive oil over a medium heat for about 5 minutes. After about 3 minutes, add the leaves (removing any tough bits of stalk), followed by the butter. Once the butter has melted, add the flour, then continue to cook for a further minute. Slowly add the milk, a little at a time, stirring constantly. Once you have a creamy sauce, remove from the heat and stir in the cheese.

Meanwhile, drizzle the bread with olive oil and season with a sprinkle of salt, then either toast in a griddle or frying pan over a medium heat, or place under the grill. Pile the cauliflower cheese on to one of the slices of toasted bread, then top with the other slice and serve as a sandwich.

Tip

Try swapping the cauliflower for broccoli – and you can switch up the Cheddar for whatever cheese you have in the fridge.

FRENCH SUMMER CHICKEN

This is sort of inspired by coq au vin, but I've taken out all the heavy ingredients and freshened it up for summer. You can make it slightly easier by just buying deboned chicken thighs, but if you do that, you'll have to sacrifice the chicken skin, which is my favourite part, so I prefer to debone them myself.

To make 1 portion

2 chicken thighs, skin on, deboned

2 bacon rashers

½ onion, sliced

Handful of frozen peas

Olive oil

Salt and pepper

To cook

Season the chicken thighs, then pan-fry, skin-side down, in a splash of olive oil over a medium heat. After about 8 minutes, flip the chicken thighs over to cook on the other side. At the same time, add the bacon and onion to the pan, giving it a stir every so often to ensure they cook evenly.

After another 8 minutes or so, once the chicken is cooked through, add the peas and a tiny splash of water and cook for another couple of minutes until everything is cooked through. Serve and enjoy.

Swap
This is a great way to use up bits and bobs of leftover veg – just throw in whatever you have lying around.

TERIYAKI TOFU

Tofu is a green and sustainable substitute for meat. Here is an idea for a teriyaki-style dish using minimal ingredients.

To make 1 portion

½ mug of basmati rice

1 mug of water

A few pieces of tofu, cut into triangles

1 tbsp honey

1 garlic clove, crushed

Pinch of dried chilli flakes

1 tbsp soy sauce

Pinch of sesame seeds

1 spring onion, thinly sliced

To cook

Put the rice and the water in a saucepan with a pinch of salt. Cover with a lid and place over a medium heat for about 7 minutes until all the water is absorbed and the rice is cooked.

Season the tofu triangles with salt and pepper, then pan-fry in a splash of sesame oil over a medium heat for a few minutes on each side. Add the honey, garlic, chilli flakes and soy sauce to the pan, along with an extra splash of sesame oil. Bring to a simmer and use the sauce this creates to baste the tofu. After a few minutes, once the tofu is a nice dark brown, remove from the pan. Sprinkle over the sesame seeds and spring onion, and serve with the rice.

Swap

For a vegan version, swap the honey for maple syrup.

DICED & ROASTED VEG LASAGNE

How do you make veg even tastier? You chop it up and roast it! By caramelising the sugars on the outside, you can elevate your veg to the next level and make this lasagne even richer in flavour. I know it's not a traditional recipe, but I like mixing things up. You'll also notice it's only got one layer: that's so you don't have to spoon half of the veg out of the dish, just to spoon it back in again.

To make 1 portion

½ onion, roughly chopped

½ carrot, roughly chopped

½ courgette, roughly chopped

½ yellow pepper, roughly chopped

Pinch of dried oregano

200g chopped tomatoes (from a 400g tin)

1 garlic clove, grated

1 fresh lasagne sheet (or precook a dry sheet in boiling water for 5 minutes)

½ ball of mozzarella, thinly sliced

Sprinkling of grated Parmesan cheese

Olive oil

Salt and pepper

To cook

Preheat the oven to 180°C/gas mark 4.

Spread the veg out on a baking tray. Season with salt, pepper and a pinch of oregano, then drizzle with a generous amount of olive oil. Roast for about 30 minutes, giving it a stir halfway through.

Transfer the roasted veg to a suitably sized ovenproof dish. Add the chopped tomatoes and grated garlic, then stir and return to the oven for another 10 minutes.

Season to taste, then top with the lasagne sheet, some slices of mozzarella and a sprinkling of grated Parmesan. Cook for another 20 minutes until the cheese is golden brown, then serve.

Swap

You can use whatever veg you have lying around for this – try it with a little aubergine or butternut squash. The key is to dice it nice and small for that caramelised flavour.

AGLIO E OLIO

Have you ever bought a whole bulb of garlic for one recipe, then only needed to use a couple of cloves? It's difficult to buy exactly what you need when garlic only comes in bulbs, so here is a tasty way to use the rest up if you have any garlic that needs finishing. The key is to add the garlic to the oil before you heat it – it will infuse as it warms up. And make sure you don't burn the garlic – that's the most common mistake.

To make 1 portion

125g spaghetti

7 garlic cloves, sliced

Pinch of dried chilli flakes

Small handful of chopped parsley

Olive oil

Salt and pepper

To cook

Cook the spaghetti in a pan of salted boiling water according to the packet instructions. Once cooked, drain and save a mugful of the cooking water.

Meanwhile, pour a very generous amount of olive oil into a cold frying pan. Add the sliced garlic and the chilli flakes. Now place the pan over a medium heat and warm until the garlic starts to fry. Once the garlic is just about to go brown, remove the pan from the heat and add the spaghetti, along with a big splash of cooking water and the parsley. Mix it all together, then season to taste and serve with an extra drizzle of olive oil.

LEEK & POTATO SAMOSAS

What do you do with leftover potatoes? Simple: make some delicious samosas for your packed lunch!

To make 1 portion (3 samosas)

½ leek, roughly chopped

Handful of roasted or boiled potatoes

1 tsp curry powder

A few sheets of filo pastry

Beaten egg, for brushing (optional)

Olive oil

Salt and pepper

To cook

Preheat your oven to 180°C/gas mark 4.

Pan-fry the leek in a splash of olive oil over a medium heat for about 5 minutes, then add the potatoes and curry powder. Season and fry for another minute or so.

Cut the filo pastry into 6 rectangles measuring about 30cm x 10cm. Arrange them so that you have 3 rectangles, each 2 sheets thick. Place 1 tablespoon of filling into the middle of each rectangle and fold the pastry around it in a triangle shape. Brush the samosas with a little oil (or some beaten egg) and place on a baking tray. Bake for about 15 minutes until golden brown. These are great hot or cold.

CIABATTA ALFREDO

My inspiration for this dish was my love of using a piece of bread to mop up those delicious flavours at the end of a meal. Call me strange, but I really think that's the best bit. You can use any bread, but I chose ciabatta because it makes the whole thing sound more Italian.

To make 1 portion

125g tagliatelle

2 garlic cloves, crushed or grated

A few slices of ciabatta

200ml single cream

Handful of grated Parmesan cheese

Handful of chopped parsley

Olive oil

Salt and pepper

To cook

Preheat your oven to 180°C/gas mark 4.

Cook the tagliatelle in a pan of salted boiling water according to the packet instructions. Once cooked, drain and save a little of the pasta water.

Meanwhile, add a generous glug of olive oil to a cold pan along with the crushed garlic and place over a medium heat. Just as the garlic begins to fry (but before it starts to colour), dip each of the ciabatta slices into the pan, then transfer to a baking tray. Place in the oven and leave to cook for 5–10 minutes until crispy and slightly charred at the edges.

Add the cream to the remaining garlic-infused oil in the pan and simmer for a few minutes, then remove from the heat. Season, then add the Parmesan and half of the parsley. Stir in the cooked pasta and a splash of the pasta cooking water, then mix in the toasted ciabatta slices and serve with the remaining parsley as a garnish.

Tip

You can use whatever kind of bread you like. This is a great way of using up bread that is starting to go a little stale.

GROUND BEEF NOODLES

Instead of breaking up the beef as you fry it, allow it to clump together a bit and get some colour on the outside: that's where the real flavour is hidden.

To make 1 portion

1 nest of noodles

100g minced beef

1 garlic clove

Pinch of dried chilli flakes

3 spring onions, roughly chopped

Splash of soy sauce

Salt and pepper

Sesame oil

To cook

Start by cooking the noodles in a pan of boiling salted water according to the instructions on the pack. Once cooked, drain and set aside.

Meanwhile, season the beef, then pan-fry in a splash of sesame oil over a high heat for about 6 minutes until nicely coloured. Add the garlic, chilli flakes and spring onions and cook for a few more minutes, then stir in the noodles. Add a splash of soy sauce, and you're done.

Tip

For a meat-free option, swap the beef for a handful of mushrooms whizzed up in a food processor to make a quick mushroom mince.

HALLOUMI CAESAR SALAD

Cooking halloumi in the oven creates a beautiful caramelisation that sort of reminds me of chicken and makes it a great alternative. The croutons in this salad add extra crunch and are a great way of using up stale bread.

To make I portion

100g halloumi, sliced

A few chunks of old sourdough bread

Pinch of dried oregano

1 tbsp mayonnaise

1 tsp Dijon mustard

A few lettuce leaves

Sprinkling of grated Parmesan cheese

Olive oil

Pepper

To cook

Preheat your oven to 180°C/gas mark 4.

Drizzle the halloumi slices with olive oil and season with pepper and oregano (you don't need salt as halloumi is already salty). Spread out on a baking tray and roast for about 15 minutes until slightly browned. Halfway through the cooking time, add the bread to the tray and turn the halloumi.

Meanwhile, in a small bowl, mix together the mayonnaise and mustard with 3 tablespoons of olive oil to create a smooth dressing.

Arrange the lettuce in a serving bowl and top with the halloumi and toasted sourdough croutons. Drizzle over some dressing and finish with some grated Parmesan and cracked black pepper.

PATCHWORK ROAST CHICKEN PIE

What do you do with all those leftover scraps of puff pastry? Simple, chuck them on top of this patchwork pie, which also features leftover roast potatoes, veg and shredded roast chicken – so it's basically a leftovers pie! If you're missing any of the ingredients listed here, you can leave them out, swap them for something else, or cook some especially for this recipe. I love this pie because the patchwork lid gives the filling a chance to bubble through, creating those gorgeous caramelised bits that you usually only get at the edges.

To make 1 portion

2 tsp plain flour

200ml milk

Handful of cooked chicken (such as roast chicken), shredded

Handful of leftover cooked veg (such as peas and carrots)

Handful of leftover cooked potatoes

1 tsp mustard (any)

Handful of grated Cheddar cheese

Leftover strips of puff pastry

1 egg, beaten (optional)

Olive oil

Salt and pepper

To cook

Preheat your oven to 180°C/gas mark 4.

Add a glug of olive oil to a saucepan, then add the flour and cook over a medium heat for 1 minute. Begin to add the milk, a little at a time, stirring continuously until a sauce forms.

Remove from the heat and throw in the chicken, veg, potatoes, mustard and cheese. If the sauce is too thick, just add a splash more milk. Season to taste, then transfer the mixture to a suitably sized ovenproof dish. Top with the pieces of puff pastry, then brush with beaten egg (if you want an extra-luxurious finish). Bake in the oven for about 30 minutes until golden brown.

> **Tip**
> For a veggie version, just leave out the chicken and add a bit more veg.

SHREDDED CHICKEN TACOS

I love tacos with slow-cooked pork shoulder, but it takes hours and hours to really break down that meat. So save some electricity (and some time!) with my much quicker chicken version, ready in about 30 minutes.

To make 1 portion

2 chicken drumsticks, skin removed

½ onion, sliced

Pinch of ground cumin

Pinch of paprika

200g chopped tomatoes (from a 400g tin)

A few soft-shell tacos or tortillas

Crumbled feta, for sprinkling

A few slices of red onion

A few sprigs of coriander

Olive oil

Salt and pepper

To cook

Season the chicken, then pan-fry over a medium heat in a splash of olive oil. After about 7 minutes, add the onion and continue to fry for a further 5 minutes. Next add the cumin, paprika and chopped tomatoes. Cook for 15–20 minutes, until the chicken is cooked through. Remove the chicken from the pan and use two forks to shred the meat from the bone. Return the shredded meat to the pan and stir through the sauce.

Load up your tacos with the chicken and tomato mixture, and top with some crumbled feta, red onion and coriander.

Tip

You can use up the rest of the tinned tomatoes in one of my other recipes – try the Pulled Chicken & Black Bean Chilli on page 60, or the Pasta Alla Norma on page 138.

GREEN VEG TOAD IN THE HOLE

I saw some mini leeks and courgettes in the supermarket and thought they'd be great for this dish, but you can easily use normal-sized veg and just chop it into chunks.

To make 1 portion

40g plain flour

1 large egg

60ml milk

2 mini leeks

2 mini courgettes

Handful of frozen peas

1 tbsp gravy granules

Salt and pepper

Olive oil

To cook

Preheat your oven to 180°C/gas mark 4.

Pour some oil into an ovenproof dish to a depth of about 1cm. Place in the oven to heat for roughly 10 minutes until the oil is smoking hot.

Meanwhile, to make the batter, mix the flour, egg and milk in a bowl with a pinch of salt. Very carefully, remove the hot dish from the oven and add the leeks and courgettes. Pour the batter into the dish and immediately return it to the oven. Bake for about 20–30 minutes until everything has risen perfectly and is a lovely golden brown colour. Don't open the oven door to check for at least the first 15 minutes.

Meanwhile, cook the peas in a pan of boiling salted water over a medium heat for about 3 minutes, then drain. Make the gravy according to the packet instructions. Serve the veggie toad in the hole with the peas, with gravy poured over the top.

Swap

This recipe will work well with most vegetables, so it's a great way of using up any different leftover veg you have.

STICKY CHUTNEY SQUASH PILAF

This isn't really a proper pilaf, but the end result looks like one. I found that the only way to get a really tasty, sticky butternut squash is to cook it separately – and the flavour boost that gives you is definitely worth the extra washing up.

To make 1 portion

¼ butternut squash, cut into 2cm cubes

1 shallot (or ½ onion), sliced into circles

2 tbsp mango chutney

½ mug basmati rice

Handful of chopped coriander

Small handful raisins

Small handful cashew nuts

Olive oil

Salt and pepper

To cook

Preheat the oven to 180°C/gas mark 4.

Spread out the butternut squash cubes on a baking tray. Season and drizzle with olive oil, then roast for about 30 minutes, adding the mango chutney and shallot halfway through and stirring to combine.

Meanwhile, put the rice and the water in a saucepan with a pinch of salt. Cover with a lid and place over a medium heat for about 7 minutes until all the water is absorbed and the rice is cooked.

Mix the rice with the sticky roasted butternut squash and shallots, then top with the chopped coriander, raisins and cashews. Season to taste and serve.

Tip

Try toasting some of the butternut squash seeds to scatter over the top. See page 120 for how to do this.

COCONUT CHICKPEA CURRY

A super simple curry using tinned chickpeas and coconut milk. If you're ever stuck for time, dig a couple of cans out of the kitchen cupboard and give this a go.

To make 1 portion

½ onion, diced

1 garlic clove, grated

1 thumb-sized piece of ginger, grated

1 tsp curry powder

1 red chilli, chopped

200g chickpeas (from a 400g tin), drained

200g coconut milk (from a 400g tin)

Small handful of chopped coriander, to serve

Olive oil

Salt and pepper

To cook

Start by pan-frying the onion in a splash of oil over a medium heat for a few minutes. Add the garlic, ginger, curry powder and half the chilli, then continue to fry for a few more minutes. Next add the chickpeas and fry for a further couple of minutes before adding the coconut milk and simmering for 5 minutes. Season to taste and serve garnished with coriander and the rest of the chilli.

Tip

This dish is easy to scale up, so you can make a bigger batch and freeze the leftovers for another time.

SAUSAGE & PEARL BARLEY HOTPOT

A warming dish topped with golden potatoes and bulked out with pearl barley. This is a great way to make a few sausages go further.

To make 1 portion

2 sausages

½ onion, roughly chopped

½ carrot, roughly chopped

Handful of pearl barley

1 chicken or vegetable stock cube

400ml water, plus extra if needed

Handful of frozen peas

leaves from 1 thyme sprig (optional)

1 potato, sliced

Olive oil

Salt and pepper

To cook

Preheat your oven to 180°C/gas mark 4.

Place the sausages on a baking tray and cook in the oven for about 25 minutes until golden brown.

Meanwhile, in a small ovenproof casserole dish, fry the onion and carrot in a splash of olive oil over a medium heat for about 7 minutes. Add the pearl barley, stock cube and water and simmer for about 20 minutes, adding more water if needed. Once cooked and about the consistency of a stew, season to taste, then add the cooked sausages, along with the peas and thyme leaves. Top with the sliced potato. Drizzle the potato slices with olive oil and season, then cook in the oven for about 20 minutes or until the potatoes are golden brown. Serve.

Tip

This is a great dish for using up any odds and ends of vegetables you have lying around.

INDEX

The right of Miguel Barclay to be identified as the author of
the work has been asserted by him in accordance with the
Copyright, Designs and Patents Act 1988.

First published in 2021
by Headline Home
An imprint of Headline Publishing Group

1

Cataloguing in Publication Data is available from the British Library

ISBN 978 1 4722 7340 6
eISBN 978 1 4722 7341 3

Commissioning Editor: Lindsey Evans
Design: Superfantastic
Photography: Dan Jones
Food styling: Bianca Nice
Food styling assistant: Dominique Alexander
Prop styling: Sarah Birks
Project editors: Kate Miles and Tara O'Sullivan
Page make-up: EM&EN
Copy editor: Tara O'Sullivan
Proof reader: Ilona Jasiewicz
Indexer: Caroline Wilding

Headline's policy is to use papers that are
natural, renewable and recyclable products and
made from wood grown in sustainable forests.
The logging and manufacturing processes are
expected to conform to the environmental
regulations of the country of origin.

Printed and bound in Germany
by Mohn Media
Colour reproduction by ALTA London

HEADLINE PUBLISHING GROUP
An Hachette UK Company
Carmelite House
50 Victoria Embankment
London EC4Y 0DZ

www.headline.co.uk
www.hachette.co.uk